CELESTIAL TRAVELER

THE AMAZING TRUE STORY OF AN ALASKAN ESKIMO'S JOURNEY INTO THE "HEREAFTER"

GLENN HERMANN

CELESTIAL TRAVELER:
THE AMAZING TRUE STORY OF AN ALASKAN ESKIMO'S JOURNEY INTO THE "HEREAFTER"
By Glenn Hermann

Copyright ©2015 Glenn Hermann
www.celestialtraveler.org

ISBN-13: 978-0-9967778-0-3

Unless otherwise indicated, all scripture quotations are taken from
THE HOLY BIBLE, NEW INTERNATIONAL VERSION®, NIV®
Copyright © 1973, 1978, 1984, 2011 by Biblica, Inc.® Used by permission.
All rights reserved worldwide.

Scripture quotations marked AMP are taken from the AMPLIFIED® BIBLE,
Copyright © 1954, 1958, 1962, 1964, 1965, 1987 by The Lockman Foundation.
Used by permission. (www.Lockman.org)

Scripture quotations marked NKJV are taken from the NEW KING JAMES VERSION®.
Copyright © 1982 by Thomas Nelson. Used by permission. All rights reserved.

Cover Design and Interior Layout by Stephen Knouse, Essqué Productions
www.essqueproductions.com

Printed in the United States of America

All rights reserved under International Copyright Law. Contents, cover, or any portion of this book may not be copied, stored, or used in whole or in part in any form without the express written permission of the author, except for brief quotations in critical reviews or articles.

~CONTENTS~

APPENDICES

This book is dedicated to...
George and Harriet (Swanson) Hermann, my dad and mom—who loved,
encouraged, and helped me become who I am. I will be forever grateful
for all they have done for me.

~ACKNOWLEDGEMENTS~

First, I am thankful to God for equipping and choosing me to write Abraham's amazing story and for His help and guidance throughout this long and challenging endeavor.

Thanks to Sharolyn, my wonderful wife of 47 years—who has been a strong encourager, excellent proofreader, and protector of my time and privacy to allow me to focus on writing.

Thanks to Sandy Holladay for her encouragement and her tireless hours of editing and formatting my text.

Thanks to Stephen Knouse for the excellent cover design and his expertise with graphics, professional formatting and getting this work press-ready. Grateful kudos also to Pat Donelson for his expertise and collaboration with Stephen on the website design.

Special thanks to my good friend, David Williams, who served as my "computer geek"—he has rescued me out of countless computer glitches while writing this book.

Thanks to Melvin Andrew, Bishop "Doc" Nicholson and Earl Samuelson for your testimonies which have been invaluable sources of information to ascertain the truth.

Thanks to Annette Hutton for her assistance with interpreting and "translating" the medical records.

Thanks to *Dragon NaturallySpeaking*—without its voice-activated technology, this book would have taken many, many more months to complete.

Thanks to Eileen George for providing important and helpful personal information and family photos.

Preface

HOW THIS BOOK CAME TO BE

On February 23, 2008, my life intersected with Abraham George's. That path-crossing has turned out to be one of those rare, once-in-a-lifetime, "Y-in-the-road" acquaintances which has affected every day of my life since. On that day, my rational mind and my belief system were jolted by the most incredible story I had ever heard, told by this Eskimo named Abraham George, from Manokotak, Alaska. He fervently proclaimed his story of having died, being taken on a journey to three celestial[1] destinations, and then being reunited with his body. I had strong reactions to it—amazement, extreme skepticism, and strong curiosity. Due to my life-long interest in the spiritual world, I was enthralled by it and drawn into a quest to determine whether what Abraham was claiming was true. I reasoned that if Abraham's story were to be found false, then he needed to be exposed as a charlatan and fraud. If, on the other hand, his claims turned out to actually be true, I felt that due to the paramount importance of its content, the entire world needed to know about it. I felt confident, due to my prior graduate training in Apologetics, that I would definitely be able to determine the truth whatever it turned out to be.

Due to my unique DNA of strong skepticism and equally strong penchant for truth, in 1975 I enrolled in and successfully completed

---

1   **Celestial** *[suh-les-chuhl]* **Adjective:** *1. pertaining to the sky or visible heaven, or to the universe beyond the earth's atmosphere, as in celestial body. 2. pertaining to the spiritual or invisible heaven; heavenly;* **Noun:** *5. an inhabitant of heaven. (Source: dictionary.reference.com) See Appendix for examples of Biblical and historical uses of celestial.*

a Master's degree in Apologetics from Harding Graduate School of Religion in Memphis, Tennessee. My purpose was to equip myself to be able to safely navigate the spirit world without being led astray. The word "*Apologetics*" is derived from the Greek word *apologia* (**literally,** "to give an answer"). Apologetics is a philosophical study of the laws of logic, rationality, and argumentation in order to differentiate truth from error and to be able to effectively communicate truth with others. Throughout Chapters 9-13 in **SECTION TWO**—MANY POWERFUL PROOFS, the phrase "**apologetic value**" recurs several times and it is to be taken as referring to the relative degree of certainty and significance of that statement or claim being made.

I ultimately made the decision to accept the challenge of putting Abraham and his testimony on trial. I committed myself to do whatever became necessary to follow the evidence trail wherever it led and to leave no stone unturned to discover the truth. That decision led me into an extensive and expensive research project including fact-finding travels to remote

Author and plane, leaving Manokotak

Alaskan villages to track down the key people who have been involved or impacted by this event and capture their first-hand testimonies. It involved countless phone interviews and procurement of medical records. My goal was to verify and document (whenever possible) every

2

significant fact surrounding this event.

I am truly grateful and honored to be the one privileged to write this book presenting Abraham George's awesome true story. It is my conviction that it is my obligation to share this astonishing and epic event with the world. May you enjoy and be enthralled by *your* journey with the *Celestial Traveler*. But be advised—exposing yourself to this material could significantly alter the remainder of your life-journey—as it has mine and numerous others.

GLENN HERMANN
AUTHOR

Introduction to
THE BOOK

Y ou are about to be taken on a journey to places terrestrial and celestial. The terrestrial journey begins in a small remote Yup'ik Eskimo village called Manokotak, on Bristol Bay in Southwestern Alaska. There you'll meet the main character, Abraham George, a rough-cut, 42-year-old Eskimo who for 20 years had the notorious reputation of being the "town drunk."

While on a routine wood gathering trip on his snow machine, Abraham had a fatal accident in which he was crushed by his sled, loaded with 1500 pounds of firewood logs. While being medevacked to a hospital in Anchorage, Alaska, his soul separated from his body and he was stunned to find himself standing in the aisle of the Learjet, gazing upon his crushed and lifeless body with four EMTs frantically working to revive it. Suddenly a dazzling celestial being appeared at his side whose face was as lightning and his human-like bodily form radiated with an intensity of light rivaling the brilliance of the noonday sun.

At that moment Abraham was transported on an astonishing journey which took him beyond the veil separating this world from the next, being guided by the awesome "Bright One." You'll hear Abraham in his own words attempting to describe the indescribable sights and experiences of his incredible celestial journey to three destinations. At the conclusion of his celestial journeys, Abraham was presented a vital message which he was to impart to mankind. He was then transported back to his mangled body on earth which was lying in an Anchorage hospital bed. It was Christmas morning, 2005. Abraham awakened to excruciating pain from head to toe. In spite of his pain, however, Abraham began immediately telling everyone—the medical staff and anyone else coming near him—about his awesome celestial experiences and urgent message.

Shortly after his arrival he was captivated by an ethereal pale blue smoke which mysteriously appeared over his bed. Abraham said its fragrance was heavenly and each time he breathed it in, he felt a strange tingling sensation which he soon realized was also reducing his pain.

For the next three days, the strange blue smoke—which only Abraham could see and smell—slowly circulated over his bed. After only three days of inhaling it, Abraham's massive injuries were healed. On December 27, 2005, he walked out of the hospital door into his new life—a life which neither he nor anyone else could ever have imagined. The second phase of Abraham's terrestrial journey begins at that moment. In this segment you'll be fascinated by angelic encounters, several head-scratching strange occurrences, and witness many lives being transformed and miraculous healings galore!

In the second half of the book—"MANY POWERFUL PROOFS"—are presented the substantial proofs which were discovered in my research that seriously impacted my view of life, death and the hereafter.

Chapter 1
A DAY OF DESTINY

You never know what a day may bring. For Abraham George—a 42-year-old rough-cut Alaskan Yup'ik Eskimo—November 29, 2005 seemed like any ordinary fall day in his remote village of Manokotak in southwestern Alaska. On that day, however, Abraham would embark on a short five mile snow machine trip to gather firewood, which would lead him on a journey to places he could never have imagined going—places earthly and celestial. That day would turn his world upside down and his life, as he had known it, would be transformed forever. For Abraham George, it was going to be his "DAY OF DESTINY."

That cold November morning Abraham awoke with his usual muddled mind and headache from his excessive drinking the night before. This was normal life for him—he'd been a chronic alcoholic for over 20 years. He had just returned the day before, from his third state-mandated alcohol treatment program. Abraham George had earned his long-standing reputation of being the "town drunk" in his home community of Manokotak, Alaska, as well as in the neighboring town of Dillingham.

> *"When I returned from the Army, I started drinking heavily until I became an alcoholic and drug addict—I was far from God."*
>
> ~ABRAHAM GEORGE

Abraham was also "meaner than a junkyard dog"—feared for his explosive violence by everyone in his village. Whenever the Alaska State Troopers flew into Manokotak to arrest Abraham George (which occurred frequently), they would always come "doubled up." This fact became a point of pride for Abraham, who with a smirk would often say *"They have to call for the backups."* He had a criminal record a mile long. A sampling of his charges from the laundry list of 37 recorded arrests include: "criminal trespass" (1997), "DWI" (1999), "disorderly conduct" (2000), "resisting arrest" (2001). His police record also characterizes him as a "menace to society."[1]

Abraham filled his mug with the strong, piping hot coffee which his wife, Eileen, had brewed for him. After adding his usual dose of canned milk and two scoops of sugar, he stepped outside to check on the weather and to finish waking up. The sky was clear that morning and the autumn air was crisp and invigorating. The sun hovered low on the southeastern horizon, as it does in western Alaska when nearing winter solstice. As he stood there savoring his morning coffee, he enjoyed listening to the cackling of ravens soaring overhead, scanning the ground for their first meal of the day. The neighborhood was buzzing from neighbors' chainsaws cutting up their winter's supply of firewood in preparation for the coming long winter. Abraham felt like it was going to be a good day.

Abraham's wife, Eileen, also Yup'ik Eskimo, is always wearing a smile. Abraham had learned, however, from their 25 years of marriage that beneath her smile was the DNA of a general. Eileen definitely "wore the pants" in the George household. When she called Abraham in for breakfast, she already had plans for his day. Abraham sat down to his preferred traditional Eskimo breakfast of dried salmon dipped in fresh seal oil and homemade white bread. On this morning there was also leftover caribou stew from the night before.

After breakfast, Eileen barked out her two-option plan for her husband's day. Abraham recalled his marching orders as: *"My wife, Eileen, told me to either go moose hunting because our freezer was empty, or go get woods for our outdoor steam bath. I decided to haul maki woods. In those days*

---

1   See Appendix for Abraham's official State of Alaska Court Records

I wasn't a believer and I smoked marijuana—on that day I had a good supply."

Maki (pronounced ma-key), is a Yup'ik term referring to their traditional native steam bath. The maki steam bath is a part of the daily routine of contemporary native village life. The maki serves two significant purposes. First, it's a cultural spiritual ritual in which the village men discuss weighty community and spiritual matters. What the women discuss is anyone's guess. The maki is also the primary means of full-body bathing

The maki experience is done in a wood structure, typically about 12' x 12'. Most of the buildings are constructed out of two-by-fours and plywood. They are furnished with simple built-in plywood sitting benches. Makis are typically heated by large homemade wood-fired barrel stoves which are encased with large stacked rocks. A large 10 to 20 gallon metal container is placed on top of the barrel stove which is then filled with water. When the stove is red-hot and the water has been heated to the perfect temperature, the bathers alternately pour water on top of the stove, rocks and themselves, using a makeshift pouring ladle made from a tin can nailed to the end of a stick. The water poured on the stove and rocks fills the room with billowing, penetrating steam. Maki room temperatures often exceed 200° F —*"The hotter the better."* The hotter the temperature combined with the amount of time a man can endure is a common bragging point among Yup'ik men—*"Real men do it hotter and endure longer."*

Author's Note:
I've enjoyed the maki experience several times myself and found it to be very refreshing and relaxing.

After eating his fill, Abraham donned his cold weather gear, grabbed his trusty Stihl chainsaw and sack lunch of dried salmon and white bread and headed out the door. After loading and securing his gear, he climbed on his well-worn green Polaris snow mobile (pronounced: "sno-go" in Yup'ik) and fired it off. He then backed it up to his homemade, 14-foot, wooden hauling sled and connected the sled's steel Y-harness to the hitch on the rear bumper of the sno-go.

It was late morning before Abraham finally pulled away from his small, plywood-sided house. The siding was weather-checked and grayed from enduring many years of wind, rain and snow without a lick of paint.

Abraham's humble home in summer - maki bath-house on left.

Abraham was heading for his recently discovered firewood spot, which had piles of downed Sitka spruce trees that had been cut a couple of years earlier to install a large TV antenna system. Only a few minutes down the trail he met up with a couple of his regular drinking buddies, who were also out to get firewood.

Author's Note: Both of Abraham's two friends are serving long-term prison sentences—one for murder, the other for rape.

The events which transpired from that point are reported by Abraham as follows:

"I caught up to them and asked, 'Where are you guys going?' They said: 'We're going after fire woods.' I told them I was going to where I went the other day near the TV antenna site, and invited them to join me and so they did. I said, 'Hey, you guys want to have a hit?' They said, 'Yes,' so we smoked it up. We were pretty stoned when we left there. When we got to my spot we cut woods for a few hours. When we were nearly finished cutting woods, I asked the younger guy to make a 'booze run' to Dillingham. He took off and was back

in less than an hour or so. The three of us started drinking and got pretty drunk."

Dillingham is about 20 trail-miles east of Manokotak. It serves as the "hub city" for Manokotak. This means that nearly all flights, all freight and supplies, come through Dillingham. Manokotak is a "dry village," (the selling or producing of alcohol is illegal), and Dillingham is "wet" (making and selling alcohol is legal). The proximity of these two villages makes "booze runs" such as this one nearly a daily activity—especially in winter, when sno-go travel is easy and fast. This ready access to alcohol is the main reason Manokotak had earned the reputation of being the most "hell-raising" village in southwestern Alaska. Alcohol is a significant contributing factor in nearly all native village crime.

By late afternoon the three drunken wood-gatherers had their sleds heaped to the max with hundreds of pounds of spruce logs. They began preparing for the five-mile journey back to Manokotak. Abraham continues his account from that moment:

"I loaded my sled with as much as I could get on it and secured the load tight. Then the weather started getting bad—it got overcast

Abraham's 14' x 4' wooden hauling sled.

11

and started snowing some real big flakes. I told the guys, 'It's time to get going.' And so we left and I was in the lead. We came to the [Kokumiak] river, which was covered with a thick layer of ice and snow. The river had long and steep banks, so I knew I needed a lot of speed to make it up the far side so I opened 'er up going down the hill. Near the bottom, my right front ski got caught under a hidden tree root which was buried under the snow. Me and my sno-go were stopped instantly, but my sled, which weighed 1,500* pounds, kept on coming. Because of the kind of hitch I had, the sled raised up and came down on top of me. I knew I was hurt bad. I was trapped under the heavy sled and was coughing up blood and having blackouts from lack of oxygen.

The other guys tried to lift the sled off me, but it was too heavy. So they unloaded the wood in order to free me. They put me on one of their sleds and brought me back to Manokotak. They didn't stop by my house, but took me straight to the medical clinic near my house."

Author's Note:
*This number is an experienced woods-man's guess, but I've determined the sled was sufficient size and strength to haul that much wood.

Abraham in front of Manokotak Clinic

When the drunken trio arrived at the Manokotak Clinic, it was already 7:30 PM and dark. The clinic was closed and the doors were locked. Nearly everyone in the village was gathered at the high school gymnasium for a basketball game.

Author's Note: Basketball games are really a big deal in Alaska village life— especially during the long cold, dark winters. Daylight is scarce and there are few exciting activities.

Melvin Andrew, VPSO, (Village Public Safety Officer) was the first to receive the emergency medical alert on his VHF radio, reporting Abraham's life-threatening accident.

Author's Note: In modern Alaska village life, the "VPSO" is the equivalent of both the town sheriff and medical authority combined. VPSOs work closely with the State Troopers and function under their authority.

Melvin was also the first medically trained person to arrive at the clinic to diagnose and treat Abraham. He recalled the details of that night, saying:

"On November 29, 2005 at approximately 7:30 PM, I received an emergency medical call, reporting that Abraham George was involved in a snow machine accident. Responding, I saw Abraham George on a homemade, wooden flat sled by the Manokotak Clinic. His two friends who brought him said that he was hurt bad, but didn't give me specific details due to their apparent intoxication. I initiated the EMS, notifying local CHAs (Community Health Aides) and attempted to get Abraham George to respond to verbal commands and physical contact. He just groaned and did not respond to commands. The local CHAs arrived and after initial assessment of Abraham George's vitals, we placed him on a hard board and brought him into the clinic. Fortunately, there was a visiting doctor in the village, Dr. Richard O'Connell, from Dillingham. O'Connell said he may have one or more rib bones broken and needed MEDEVAC."

Melvin Andrew called for the emergency medevac plane from Dillingham. The plane's arrival was delayed for about an hour due to the blizzard conditions raging in both Dillingham and Manokotak.

Abraham continued coughing up blood and drifted in and out of consciousness. Finally at about 8:30 PM, weather conditions improved enough for the fixed-wing aircraft to take off from Dillingham and 15 minutes later it touched down on Manokotak's snow-covered gravel runway.

Manokotak's gravel airstrip in winter.

The following are Abraham's recollections of his time at the clinic: *"They checked me and could tell my blood pressure was very low and falling. They determined that I was likely going to die from internal bleeding if I didn't get to medical help soon. So they called for a plane to take me to the hospital in Dillingham. It was snowing hard so the plane was delayed…the plane finally made it into Manokotak."*

V.P.S.O. Andrew continues reporting on the severity of Abraham's medical condition: *"Abraham George was dying a slow death. The local pastor, John Nicore, arrived at the clinic and prayed for Abraham. Abraham George's daughter, Karla, came in and asked him to use holy water. The local CHAs and the doctor kept timely vitals of Abraham George [while waiting for the planes arrival]—each time their facial expressions and words grew worse."*

Sally Nukwak was one of the CHAs who Melvin had summoned to assist with Abraham's emergency care. Sally had this to say regarding Abraham's medical condition while at the clinic: *"I was one of the health aides who assisted when Abraham had his accident and I thought he wouldn't make it due to the severity of his injuries."*

Melvin continues his eyewitness account from the time of the plane's arrival: *"Finally, the EMS plane arrived. We loaded Abraham George into the plane. By this time his vitals were erratic and clearly not far from death. As soon as the plane took off, I told the person next to me that, 'He is not coming home alive, but in a casket.' I was heart-broken for his children and wife, but deep inside I was happy he was not coming back; one less 'bad boy' to watch and deal with."*

Upon arrival at Kanakanak Hospital in Dillingham, Abraham was rushed into the x-ray department to assess his internal injuries. After a battery of x-rays were taken, a nurse wheeled Abraham into an adjacent room. Two physicians stood before the x-ray screen interpreting and discussing Abraham's condition and prognosis. What they saw was alarming— "Seven fractured ribs on his right side, two fractured vertebrae, broken collar bone, fractures to pelvis and tail-bone, punctured and collapsed right lung,"

MEDICAL RECORDS INTERPRETATION
IN LAYMAN'S TERMS

FRACTURE ILIUM- BROKEN PELVIC GIRDLE BONE
BRACHIAL PLEXUS INJURY- DAMAGED NERVE SPINE
FRACTURE SACCRUM/COCCYX-BROKEN TAILBONE
LIVER LACERATION-TEARING OF ORGAN WITHOUT CUTTING

PNEUMOHEMOTHORAX- *AIR AND BLOOD ESCAPED IN TO CHEST CAVITY*

FRACTURED RIBS X SEVEN- *BROKEN RIB CAGE BONES*

FRACTURE LUMBAR VERTEBRA- BROKEN BACK BONE
ACUTE RESPIRATORY FAILURE- FAILURE TO BREATHING FUNCTION
PNEUMONIA- INFECTION OF LUNGS
HEMATURIA- BLOOD IN URINE
SUBQUTANEOUS EMPHYSEMA-AIR TRAPPED UNDER SKIN
ALCOHOL ABUSE-DRUNK-CHRONIC CONDITION
PLEURAL EFFUSION- WATER AROUND LUNGS
POST HEMORRAGHIC ANEMIA- ANEMIA DUE TO BLOOD LOSS
LUNG CONTUSION- BRUISED LUNG TISSUE
FRACTURE SCAPULA- BROKEN COLLAR BONE
FOREIGN BODY BRONCHUS- ABNORMAL LUNG FINDINGS
CONTUSION ABDOIMINAL WALL- BRUISED BELLY
HIGH BLOOD PRESSURE- CHRONIC CONDITION
ASTHMA- CHRONIC LUNG CONDITION-
TOBACCO ABUSE-CIGARETTE SMOKER

Interpreted by Annette Hutton, Coding Specialist
(30 years of medical record work experience)

As Abraham lay there drifting in and out of consciousness, he distinctly recalls overhearing one of the doctors mumbling: *"This guy isn't going to make it.*" He was gripped with fear as he contemplated being on the edge of an uncertain eternity.

The Kanakanak Hospital attending medical staff quickly determined that due to the extent and severity of Abraham's injuries, he needed to be medevacked immediately to Anchorage. The medical transfer form reads: "*Based on the reasonable risks and benefits to the patient it is determined that the medical benefits of medical treatment at another medical facility, outweigh the increased risks of transport.*" This was signed by the attending physician, who immediately called for a medevac Learjet to transport Abraham to the better-equipped Alaska Native Medical Center in Anchorage.

Abraham's recollections continue from when the Aero-Med Learjet landed at the Dillingham airport: "*The jet finally reached Dillingham [at approximately 1:30 AM on November 30th]. They rushed me down to the airport to medevac me to Anchorage. The four EMTs put me inside the little plane. They secured my stretcher and we were on our way.*"

BRISTOL BAY HEALTH CORPORATION-MANOKOTAK CLINIC 11/29/2005 1915 HRS ACCIDENT 1855 HRS TRANSFERRED 2119

Primary First responders at the scene of the accident.

Stabilized, level of consciousness INTOXICATED and transported by MEDIVAC to KANAKANAK HOSPITAL.ARRIVED 2316 11/29/2005

Admitted to hospital for* LEVEL 2* trauma evaluation :Reported Mental Status Changes due to level of intoxication no mention of COMA

*Facilty with Inpatient diagnostic services such as RADIOLOGY, OPERATIING ROOM

Transported to ANMC via AEROMED at 1335 HRS 11/30/2005 (NO RECORD OF FLIGHT CARE)

ANNETTE HUTTON CODING SPECIALIST
30 YEARS OF MEDICAL RECORD WORK EXPERIENCE

Bristol Bay Health Corp. accident record.

In a few moments the Aero Med jet reached cruising altitude and was making a 450 mile-an-hour beeline for Anchorage, about 350 miles to the northeast. Abraham was hooked up to an array of life-support apparatus. Shortly after takeoff, Abraham's only functioning lung shut down, bringing on "acute respiratory failure."

"When that happened, it seems like I fell asleep; then it seems like I got up from my body. My body was in pain, but when I got up from my stretcher I left the pain in my body. My soul was standing next to my body. I saw myself lying on the stretcher and these four EMTs working on me. I still had all my senses—I still could see, hear, taste and smell. I heard one EMT saying, 'Let's not administer CPR, we might inflict more injuries—His ribs are too busted up.' Then they put that shocking tool—looks like jumper cables—on my chest. When they put a shock to my heart, I saw my chest went up and went down. They did that four times. I saw a heart monitor right above my body. I could still hear—I heard that really high-pitched sound that means my heart stopped, I think. Then another EMT said: 'Let's give him one more try.' Suddenly, someone was standing right next to me on my right side. He was a man figure, but he was so full of light—he was so bright—I couldn't see his face."

~ABRAHAM GEORGE

SECTION ONE

CELESTIAL TRAVELS

Introduction to
Section One

"People consistently have wanted to know more…always more."
~Don Piper
Author "90 Minutes in Heaven"

Chapters 4 through 7 present Abraham's account of his astonishing speed-of-thought celestial travels to heaven, outer darkness, hell, return to heaven, and finally his return to reunite with his body on earth.

If you're like me, you want to learn everything about each place Abraham visited and every sight he saw on the "other side." I have made a full-scale effort to capture every detail of his experience through barraging Abraham with questions. During our first interview, he bluntly told me: *"My dad and grandpa taught me that it's not polite to ask personal questions and it makes me angry when people do!"* At the risk of agitating him further, I boldly responded: *"You'll have to get over it, because if you don't answer my questions, you'll be answering questions like mine for thousands of other people the rest of your life."* The content of the following four chapters is a compilation of Abraham's own words from his publicly given testimony and the additional information derived from numerous personal interviews in which I probed deeper into the details of the things he described in his public testimony.

The scope and parameters of Abraham's celestial travels were not random. They followed a predetermined agenda of the One who invited and guided him through the entirety of his celestial journeys. Everything he was shown was purposeful and was connected to a significant truth he was to grasp and carry back within him to tell the world. Abraham clarified this, saying: *"Just like the blinking of an eye, he took me places… it was all by His command—I had no control. He showed me what he wants me to see. There are so many things that He showed me, but these are the most important for me to tell. He didn't show me everything—just a little peek or corner of it. He showed me enough for me to believe there's heaven and hell."*

Abraham's celestial experiences seemed also to be episodic, with each changing episode being introduced by the Yup'ik word "Atam," which translates, *"Look! Take a look at this. Look here. Pay attention to this."* Whenever Abraham heard *"Atam,"* it was his cue to cease his fixation on all the astonishing glory and wonders of heavenly scenes surrounding him and to re-focus on what he was about to be shown, or to become aware of the things in heaven which are vitally important to Jesus. *"Everything that he showed me, he'd say, "Atam—look."* Each episode was also full of meaning with meaning and accompanied by interpretive instruction and nearly always with recurring core messages, such as: *"Tell my children I am the way and the truth and the life."* If significance were to be determined solely by repetition, then this statement, which was repeated multiple times throughout his celestial travels, is the primary message given to Abraham.

Chapter 2

ENCOUNTER WITH THE "BRIGHT ONE"

Abraham was stunned by the dazzling celestial being who suddenly appeared at his right side as he was standing in the aisle of the medevac Learjet. He turned his head for a closer look. He was astonished by the intensity of the brightness of the light which was emanating from Him. His face was as lightning and his bodily form rivaled the brilliance of the noonday sun. Abraham thought it surprising that even though the light was so intense, he was still able to make out a human-like bodily form. Abraham exclaimed: *"He was a man figure, but he was so bright, so bright, I couldn't see his face."*

Abraham, not knowing who or what this presence was, referred to him simply as: *"the Bright One."*

At that moment, Abraham recalled feeling: *"unworthy, unclean, and ashamed."* Then unexplainably these feelings vanished—being displaced by overwhelming sensations of love, joy, and peace which were emanating simultaneously from the "Bright One" standing beside him. Abraham explained: *"This person who was standing next to me was full of love, full of joy and full of peace. He had all of those at the same time. I felt love, joy, and peace from him. I didn't know who he was but I wanted to be next to him."*

Abraham's next shocking experience was when the enthralling "Bright One" began speaking to him in perfect Yup'ik, his native tongue. *"This person, right next to me, was speaking to me in my Yup'ik language. I thought, 'How could he know my Yup'ik language?' I was amazed!"* But before he could even utter a word, the "Bright One" responded instantly to his thought saying: *"I know all the languages of the world."* Abraham was overwhelmed! *"To me it was amazing that he knew my thoughts, because when I was living, no one would ever know my thoughts."*

Abraham was beside himself with curiosity and wonder as to who this awesome and mysterious being might be and what this extraordinary visitation meant. Though he had the bodily appearance of a man, Abraham perceived that he was much more. The true identity of this awe-inspiring being was soon to be revealed to him.

Then Abraham was asked the most stunning question of his entire life—*"Do you want to see where the saved souls go?"* The instant he had the thought that he did, Abraham found himself standing in a bright and glorious place with the Bright One still beside him.

Chapter 3
WHO IS ABRAHAM GEORGE?

braham's fondest memories growing up as an Alaskan native were the three seasonal subsistence camps—spring, summer, and fall. During these special harvest seasons, native families made an all-out effort to harvest sustenance from the land and water to fill their larder for the entire year.

There are several highlights of Abraham's subsistence camp memories. Foremost was the long riverboat rides to and from the camps on the wild and winding Kuskokwim River. There were many aspects of those exciting boat trips which marked his memory—the wonder of the pristine wilderness shouldering the shores of the river and the exciting anticipation of catching glimpses of unsuspecting beavers, otters, bears, or moose carrying on their daily life routines. He fondly recalls the playful wrestling matches with his younger brothers, Robert and Joe, on the natural carpet of spongy green muskeg. Especially memorable was the evening campfire ritual. Abraham and family would end their days sitting on rough-hewn stumps, soaking up the soothing warmth of blazing campfires. It was around those camp fires that the young boy Abraham was entertained and enthralled by the thrilling tales told by his father and grandfather—tales of wild outdoor adventures, of face-to-face bear encounters, trophy moose and caribou kills, and net-breaking salmon catches. Subsistence camp also provided the added excitement of sleeping out in canvas tents or in one of the rustic sod-roofed log hunting cabins.

Spring camp began in early April, while the winter's snow still blanketed the ground, and lasted through breakup, which usually took place from mid-to-late May. By springtime, food supplies were normally meager and Abraham's family harvested anything edible. The larder typically would include some or all of the following: caribou, bear, snowshoe hares, beavers, muskrats, ducks, geese, grouse and ptarmigan. Travel for spring subsistence camp in those days was primarily by dogsled, but also required travel by water after breakup.

Summer camp or "fish camp" began upon the arrival of the first run of spawning salmon to the family fish site about 75 miles up the Kuskokwim River from the ocean. The focus of summer camp was harvesting the abundant runs of salmon—kings, reds, dogs and silvers. The season began in mid-June and continued until the salmon run tapered off in mid-to-late August.

TRADITIONAL NATIVE PRESERVING METHODS

Salmon and game meat from the land were processed and preserved by the Eskimo women in several traditional native ways. Most of the salmon and game meat was air dried because it was the quickest and simplest way of preserving meat. The drying process involved cutting the flesh into strips and then hanging them on open-air drying racks. These teepee shaped racks were made out of all-natural materials on hand. The support frames were constructed from small tree trunks. The cross members were made of long spindly limbs which were crudely bound to the framework using flexible young twigs.

Some of the salmon catch was preserved by utilizing the naturally occurring permafrost layer underground. "Permafrost" is a subsurface layer of frozen earth which never thaws and is found over most of the northern half of Alaska. Caverns were hand-dug down to the permafrost layer (which normally is less than 2 feet). The salmon catch would then be placed into the hollowed-out area and covered with a blanket of tundra moss, which is an effective insulator. This was probably man's

Artwork depicting an Alaskan Native summer fishing camp
"Summer Camp", by Ken Lisbourne, Pt. Hope, Alaska 2008 (Used by permission)

first all-natural, perfect refrigerator. "Salting" was yet another common method for preserving a portion of the catch. This offered the advantage of portability. For this process the salmon fillets were heavily salted and then packed into wooden barrels in alternating layers of fish and salt. Most of these preserving methods are still in use today.

Between salmon catches, the women and children ventured onto the tundra (bears permitting), and picked wild blueberries, salmon berries, and low-bush cranberries. The berries would be quickly rendered into jams and sauces with sugar. A portion of the berries would frequently be made into "Eskimo ice cream," called "akutaq" (pronounced "a-goo-tuk"). This was the camp favorite. This gourmet native dessert was made with equal parts of fresh berries, sugar, and Crisco. "Akutaq" is still very popular in the Eskimo villages of northern and western Alaska and is always one of the featured entrées at any native gathering involving food.

Fall hunting camp occurred from August through freeze-up in mid-to-late November. Hunting camp was Abraham's favorite because the focus was on harvesting the prized moose and caribou. It strongly resonated with his "hunter-gatherer" DNA. Autumn's frost also brought an end to the swarms of billions of bloodthirsty mosquitoes and the array of other irritating biting insects which thrive on the swampy tundra throughout Alaska's brief summer. The eradication of insects brought relief to man and beast from their incessant torment. The pungent aroma of fermenting leaves, plants and berries was another pleasant memory of Abraham's fall camp experiences. Last, but certainly not least, were his fond recollections of Alaska's spectacular autumn beauty when tundra and mountains are transformed into a natural tapestry of scarlet, magenta, bright yellow, and fiery orange. This beauty will be forever etched in his memory of fall camp.

Abraham always felt a deep sense of fulfillment and gratitude as he and his family journeyed home from a productive subsistence hunt—heavily laden with the precious sustenance from the land. For Abraham this was life as it should be. He understood that harvesting success meant that his family would have sufficient food to survive Alaska's long and cold winter.

FAMILY HERITAGE

Abraham was born to Jesse and Mary George, indigenous Yup'ik Eskimos[1], on March 26, 1962, in Akiachak, a small Yup'ik Eskimo village located on the Yukon/Kuskokwim River Delta in western Alaska. Akiachak, as all Alaskan native villages, had and still maintains a purely subsistence lifestyle.

Abraham received his now-popular nickname "Ipli" from his Grandma George who, according to family tradition, was unable to pronounce "Abraham" in English. Whenever she attempted to, it would always come out, "Ipli-ham." This eventually became shortened to "Ipli." This nickname is now used by family and friends as often as his birth name.

---

1   The Yup'ik are a group of indigenous peoples of western, southwestern, and south-central Alaska and the Russian Far East. Alaska Yup'ik (plural Yupiit) comes from the Yup'ik word yuk meaning "person" plus the post-base -pik meaning "real" or "genuine." Thus, it literally means "real people." The majority of archaeologists believe the Yup'ik to have migrated from eastern Siberia. As of the 2000 U.S. Census, the Yup'ik population in the United States numbered over 24,000, of whom over 22,000 lived in Alaska. (Source: Wikipedia)

Abraham attended the BIA (Bureau of Indian Affairs) school in Akiachak. For Abraham, schoolwork was drudgery because to him it didn't relate to "real life" and his pragmatic core-value—"if something had neither fur nor scales, its value was questionable." He graduated from BIA school in 1979, with an overall "C" average. Native customs and ways were deeply instilled into Abraham from his youth. He had the unique experience of growing up with grandparents living next door—one on each side of his house. This gave Abraham the advantage of learning subsistence skills from both of two grandpas and his dad—all lifelong experienced survivalists, hunters and commercial fishermen.

A NATIVE "DENNIS THE MENACE"

Ipli was a native variation of "Dennis the Menace" as a youth. Due to the fact that he spent lots of time with his Grandpa John Wassilie (his mother's dad), he developed a special bonding to him. This privileged bonding unfortunately positioned Grandpa Wassilie to be the brunt of several of his grandson's mischievous pranks. Ipli, with grinning face, delights in retelling the episode when he happened upon his grandpa Wassilie passed out on the sofa from intoxication. A naughty scheme flashed across his mind. He quickly and stealthily snatched the syrup bottle from the kitchen cupboard and spread a thin coating over grandpa's closed eyelids. When his grandpa awoke the next morning he was unpleasantly surprised to discover that his eyelids were glued shut. He groped blindly to find the sink to wash the sticky crust from his eyelids and restore his sight. Abraham tells of another occasion when on a cold wintry day he locked his grandpa in the outhouse. Any disciplinary repercussions suffered by Abraham have never been mentioned.

RELIGIOUS HERITAGE

Anyone born in Akiachak at that time as well as anyone else living in the village with religious leanings became "Moravians" as a matter of course. Abraham's parents and grandparents were no exception. The following are Abraham's recollections of his religious heritage: *"My parents and grandparents believed in the Lord. They prayed, read the Bible, and took me to church all the time. Whenever they spoke to me about heaven and hell I used to tell them, 'I don't think there's heaven and I don't think there's hell.'"* As soon as Abraham completed high school, he departed from his family's spiritual path. He cut church attendance to a mere few times per year which he admitted: *"was only for show."* On Sunday mornings, it made more sense to the young Ipli to head into the woods, brandishing his bolt-action .22 rifle to hunt rabbits or ptarmigan, than to sit through another boring sermon. As Abraham grew older, his disdain for religion also increased. To him, religion was a meaningless interference to life. Abraham summarized his spiritual condition at that time saying: *"In my old life I never was very religious. Even though I was brought up in a Christian home, I never used to read the Bible. I never really was a Christian. I was far from God."*

MILITARY CAREER

At 22 years of age, Abraham enlisted in the Army National Guard. While in the Guard he formed relationships with the wrong crowd. The influence of this new peer group led Abraham on a downward path into both alcohol and marijuana use which eventually developed into strong addictions. Though Ipli had earned the rank of Sergeant E-5 during his enlistment, his substance abuse eventuated into a "less-than-honorable" discharge in 1997. Abraham was 35 years old when he returned to Akiachak. His addictions

*Abraham George - Army National Guard
Served 1984-1997*

followed him home and continued to grow worse. They were to have profound and long-term destructive consequences in his life and family.

WEDDING BELLS

At fish camp in the summer of 1997, Ipli met and fell in love with Eileen Gloko, who became his wife on November 22 of that year. Within several months, Abraham and his new bride moved from the village of Akiachak to Manokotak, where they still reside today. In Manokotak, Eileen gave birth to their four children: Karla, Allison, Amber, and Jeffrey.

Abraham and Eileen George's wedding, Nov. 22, 1997

Abraham and Eileen with children Karla, Allison, Amber, & Jeffrey

The Town Drunk

Following the move to Manokotak, Abraham's life continued to spiral downward. He became a hard-core alcoholic and drug addict:

> *"When I returned from the Army, I started drinking heavily until I became an alcoholic and drug addict."*
>
> ~ABRAHAM GEORGE

After several more years of alcohol abuse Abraham became known as the "town drunk" in both Manokotak and neighboring Dillingham. A long-time acquaintance of Abraham's, Sirena Tennyson, from Dillingham, shared her memories about Abraham's life during those years: *"I've known Abraham 10+ years. I knew him as a local fisherman. He was the 'downtown drunk.' He was arrested for criminal activity and drinking numerous times."*

During this period, Abraham's wife, Eileen, also fell prey to alcohol's clutches. Now both of them were "on the skids" and hopelessly descending into lives of increasing chaos, pain, and trouble. Moses Ayojiak, a longtime friend of Abraham and Eileen, shared his observations of their lives at that time:

> *"Abraham used to fight with his wife; they were drunks."*
>
> ~MOSES AYOJIAK
> *TOGIAK, ALASKA*

Abraham and Eileen degenerated to the point where their alcohol cravings and drug addictions drove them into bouts of abandoning their children. They began taking turns traveling to the neighboring town of Dillingham for hard-core drinking binges lasting from several days to several weeks. At times they would both leave their children unattended for drinking binges together. During those dark and turbulent years they nearly lost their children to Alaska Child Protection Services several times.

Ken and Sally Nukwak, neighbors of the Georges for many years, shared their over-the-fence observations of their lifestyle during this time:

"They'd be out of town for days at a time [on drinking binges] and it got to a point where they would both be gone. I wouldn't call him a productive citizen."

~KEN NUKWAK

"Before his accident, Abraham and his wife, Eileen, would take turns having drinking binges for a week to nearly a month, away from their kids. I would either see him or his wife drunk in Dillingham. I was sickened at times due to his behavior and remarks he made while drunk."

~SALLY NUKWAK

THE BADDEST MAN IN TOWN

Abraham continued to regress into a hopeless cycle of alcohol binges, marijuana highs, recurrent fighting and frequent arrests. He was simultaneously becoming more violent and abusive in his home life and in public. His wife lamented that Abraham had frequently abused her verbally and physically, leaving her at times with black eyes and multiple bruises all over her body. Their marriage was painful and disintegrating at the time of Abraham's fateful accident in 2005. Eileen confessed that when she received word of her husband's accident: *"I was hoping that he would die!"* (A sentiment which was shared by others in Manokotak.) Abraham spoke of the pattern of his life at that time as: *"I was mostly fighting."* Melvin Andrew, who in 2005 had been Manokotak's VPSO for twenty years, expressed his bitter sentiments toward Abraham as follows: *"Abraham George was a law-breaker, a drunk, and an all-around nemesis of police officers. I have had several encounters with Abraham George. In one incident I have had to use pepper spray and a baton to subdue him while effecting an arrest. He was intoxicated, of course. We hog-tied him to transport him to the holding facility. He often called me all kinds of offensive names when in verbal distance and offensive sign language otherwise. I was happy that he was hurt that day—one less bad boy to watch. Abraham George's criminal history says it all."* [2]

Abraham George was dreaded by Melvin and the Alaska State Troopers.

---

2 *See page 183 for copy of official court records.*

Whenever they flew into Manokotak to arrest him (which was often), they always came doubled up. Abraham said: *"The cops couldn't get me one-on-one—they have to call for backups."* On the occasion of one of his arrests, he astonishingly tore the handcuffs apart.

Prior to his accident in 2005, Abraham had racked up an extraordinary criminal record of 37 arrests. A small sampling of his arrest record includes: "Criminal Trespass, DWI, Disorderly Conduct, and Resisting Arrest." His criminal record also characterized Abraham as: *"a menace to society."*

This is the man—Abraham George—whose amazing story this book is about—he is the CELESTIAL TRAVELER.

Chapter 4
GLORY OF HEAVEN

ABRAHAM'S ASTONISHING SIGHTS, EXPERIENCES, & FEELINGS WHILE IN HEAVEN

braham's celestial travels began with a thought. As he stood in the aisle of the Learjet and pondered the most incredible question he had ever been asked—*"Do you want to see where the saved souls go?"* Abraham said: *"In the twinkling of an eye, he brought me inside this beautiful place. I was amazed by the brightness—it was so bright! On earth a sunny day is dark compared… the brightness lights up everything and everything is glowing. Right away I looked for the sun. There was no sun and no shadows. As soon as I thought, 'How can this be?' he answered my thought and told me—'This place is lit by God's glory.'*

"Everything up in heaven is hard to explain because the beauty of that place cannot be explained in words. Everything is not like here on earth. Everything is much more clear than here on earth. Everything has more to it. Everything has more color. Everything was inviting. I could see my hands, my knees and my feet—I was talking normal, but my senses were keener, more clear. Colors were brighter, deeper, richer, fuller. Everything was inviting. Everything in heaven is alive and full of God's glory, and you are drawn by everything.

"From where I was standing everything looked like pure, pure sparkling gold, like the glow of a sunset. Then I knew this place was heaven."

Abraham's sensations of love, joy, and peace which had abided with him ever since his encounter with the "Bright One" on the jet, were suddenly intensified upon his arrival in Heaven. Abraham described it as heaven's atmosphere: *"Up in heaven there's indescribable peace, joy and love. It was like I was breathing in more love, joy, and peace with each breath. God's presence is everywhere and in everything. It was the most wonderful feeling I have ever had."*

THE IDENTITY OF THE "BRIGHT ONE" REVEALED

"On the jet I didn't know who the 'Bright One' was, but I felt peace, joy and love from him and wanted to be close to him." As Abraham pondered the identity of the astonishingly bright being who had been his constant companion and celestial guide, he suddenly heard him speak in perfect Yup'ik: *"I am the way, and the truth, and the life. No man comes to the Father but by me."* That statement flashed a childhood memory of a Sunday school lesson about Jesus when Abraham was about seven years old. Ipli recalled his teacher emphasizing that Jesus was "the way, the truth, and the life." At that moment his mind was opened. Abraham recalled: *"Now I knew the 'Bright person' was Jesus! I knew he was my savior. Suddenly, I felt like a dirty rag—unworthy to be in his presence. I felt ashamed of my past and knew I had no right as a sinner to stand before Him and talk to Him. At the same time I felt peace, joy and love and great calmness. Deep inside I felt He cared very much about me. I was so at peace. He was so awesome, so bright! All the colors of the rainbow were around Him. I still couldn't see his face—it was too bright! To me it was God's glory. I saw nail prints in His hands and his feet. They looked like open holes, like piercing—they were very apparent. When Jesus spoke to me it would come nice and clear for me to understand. With His voice came peace, joy and then love—all three at once."*

Author's Note: All communication with Abraham took place in his native Yup'ik language. He said the angels also spoke to him in fluent Yup'ik.

Abraham continues: *"Everything happened at Jesus' command. He had enormous power. The power of Jesus is so awesome that nobody could*

36

imagine it here on earth. Every time when He spoke, it instantly happened. I had no control, but never felt scared. It was all by His command. He took me places— just like blinking of an eye. Time didn't matter. The next thing—we were there!"

Author's Note: Abraham's travels were instantaneous— "like blinking of an eye; time didn't matter. You are thinking of something and you are there already." Abraham said there was no consciousness or awareness of time passing. It appears that spiritual travel in the hereafter will be at the incomprehensible speed of thought.

THE THRONE OF GOD

"Again Jesus said: 'Atam!' Then I saw a glorious throne with a bright figure on it. From where I was standing the throne looked like it was about twelve feet high. That place was full of bright smoke like a bright fog around the throne—real powerful smoke. I can't describe it with words. There were also all the colors of the rainbow, only they were keener than on earth. I saw lightning and heard loud thunder. To me it was God the Father's glory. Everything in heaven moves by the glory of God. Everything was in harmony and everything was alive."

Author's Note: Abraham stated that after he was reunited with his body, a similar ethereal, heavenly smoke mysteriously appeared above his hospital bed.

THE PRAISE & WORSHIP SURROUNDING GOD'S THRONE

"Around the throne there were four huge, bright angel-like beings—one posted on each corner. There was also one flying above the throne—he was the loudest. They had many eyes and each had six wings—upper, middle, lower. The upper wings would cover their faces, lower wings would cover their feet, and with the middle wings they would fly up and down, worshiping. As one went up, another one would go down—nonstop. They would sing: 'Holy, holy, holy, Lord God Almighty.' They were praising God with sounds like echoes. One would echo to the other nonstop, back and forth. Then I saw and heard angels singing: 'Holy, holy, holy is the Lord God Almighty who has been forever.' All the holy angels and the saved souls at the same time worshipped God the Father in perfect harmony.

"Everything up in heaven moves whenever God is praised—even the grass and flowers move in harmony. Every saved soul (including babies, who died in childbirth or infancy or had been aborted) was raising their arms and praising Almighty God."

THE HEAVENLY ANGELS

"Again Jesus said: 'Atam!' Then I looked and saw so many angels. They were so awesome! They were all so bright. They were all different. Some had wings like swans, some like giant eagles, and some didn't have wings at all. They were different sizes—some were huge; some were the size of humans. They had hair and color of skin. They talked to me in Yup'ik. Jesus said: 'They, too, know all the languages of the earth'. He told me angels have different assignments. Some are guardian angels, some warring angels, some ministering angels, and some comforting angels' They wore angel garments—different from clothes. They were all glorifying our heavenly Father. The angels' singing was out of this world! They take turns when they sing. Some sing this one verse and then the other angels sing the same verse back. I never heard sounds like that ever, ever in my whole life. The music was very professional sounding. It was most beautiful and words can't describe it."

Author's Note: "Professional" was the closest word in Abraham's, then very limited, English vocabulary to describe the grandeur of the music.

THE PLANTS IN HEAVEN

"In heaven I saw green grass, beautiful flowers, many other bigger green plants and trees. The grass was three inches long and was so green you could feel it. Jesus told me: 'Green is the color of life and everything up there is alive'. It was not like earthly grass. I was drawn to the grass and wanted to touch it, so I kneeled down and put my fingers in the grass—it felt soft to me and then the grass wrapped around them and hugged my fingers! I felt life, peace, joy and love coming from the grass and it went way down inside me. It made me tingle all over!

"There were many varieties and colors of beautiful flowers. Even if you pick

a petal it will not die. The colors were brighter and were much, much prettier than flowers on earth. The flowers were everywhere, like a paradise. It was hilly and they stretched out as far as I could see. Whenever the heavenly beings with the six wings glorified the Heavenly Father, saying: 'Holy, holy, holy, is the Lord God Almighty,' all the plants started sparkling like diamonds and moved at the same time in harmony. They burst with wonderful smells. Each kind had their own smell. No smell that I've ever smelled before on earth can compare to it and words can't explain it. It's not of the earth—it is heavenly!

Author's Note: Abraham reports that this same heavenly aroma occasionally manifests in his ministry, especially when he is praying for someone's healing. When it does, healings always occur. Once, I faintly smelled it myself while making hospital calls with Abraham—it was a very captivating and pleasant fragrance.

"The trees were brighter and their colors were more beautiful than on earth—colors I can't describe with words. The trees had mostly green leaves. Jesus said: 'They are for the healing of the nations.' On each side of the river of life I saw twelve trees. Jesus answered my thought and said: 'These are the trees of life. Each month they grow new fruits.' Each tree had different kinds of fruit on it. I saw apples, bananas, oranges, plus kinds I didn't know. I even saw—seems like diamond trees—they sparkled like diamonds. The bark, branches and leaves were real glittery. I was amazed!"

A CRYSTAL-CLEAR RIVER

"Again Jesus said: 'Look (Atam)!' Then he showed me this crystal clear river. The water was moving and glowing. I never saw in my whole life water as clear. Our water [Alaska's pristine wilderness water] is dirty compared to it. You could see right through like it was glass. I felt like jumping in, but I had to follow him. Right underneath the water I saw glowing just like it was gold. Then I thought, 'Where does this river come from?' Jesus answered my thought: 'This river is from my Father's throne.'"

THE HEAVENLY MANSIONS

"Then Jesus said: 'Atam!' Then he showed me mansions as far as I could see. I thought: 'What are these?' Jesus answered my thought: 'These are the mansions for my children—the saved souls—to receive as their home, because they have accepted me as their personal Savior. These mansions were not made by human hands but by the glory of God.' Everything about them is different from on earth. They looked like they were made out of gold. I saw diamond trimming and pure gold—diamonds and precious stones everywhere. Their beauty is greater than words can describe. Every mansion had the name of the person who will live in it. Jesus said: These mansions were not made by human hands. I was wondering what the inside looked like and instantly Jesus took me inside one of those mansions. I didn't see any lights, but everything was bright inside and there were no shadows. Everything was sparkling like diamonds and lit by the glory of God, which was everywhere in there. I saw different sized rooms and very, very expensive furniture. It seemed like it was made with ivory and handles out of pure gold. The floor of that mansion was gold like glass."

THE WALLS AND STREETS IN HEAVEN

"Then Jesus showed me walls that stretched as far as I could see. They looked like they were made out of marble or some kind of special stone. I saw twelve gates. There were three on each side. I saw the names of the apostles on each gate. There were two giant angels with wings, holding big swords on each side of the gates. The gates looked like the inside of a clam, only brighter.

"Then I saw golden streets that you could see right through—that's how clear they were. I kneeled down and touched the street and it felt very hard. It was so awesome!"

THE SOULS ABRAHAM MET IN HEAVEN

"Then Jesus said: 'Look—these are the saved souls.' Everywhere I saw these saved souls wearing white, white, white garments—seems like gowns— but when I looked closer at them it seems like there was this bright light

moving on and in their garments like a wind was blowing on them, But there wasn't any wind!"

EVERYONE IS YOUNG IN HEAVEN

Abraham continues: *"I met many people in heaven I knew who were old when they passed away. The first person I met in heaven was this old lady that we buried in Manokotak the day before my accident [November 28, 2005]. Her name was Balakea John. She was a very kind and devoted Christian. She would always walk to church no matter what the weather was. She was very old when she died, probably in her 80's. When I saw her in heaven I couldn't believe my eyes—she had wavy black hair. Seems like bright fog was moving on and in her garments. She looked very young and was so beautiful!*

Author's Note: The phrase "Look—these are the saved souls," recurs multiple times throughout Abraham's escorted tour of heaven. It is the author's opinion that Jesus was, by this, clarifying His true passion and what, to Him, is of supreme value in heaven—"the saved souls of men." This explanation is supported by Jesus' personal definition of heaven as: "the place where the saved souls go."

"Then I saw this guy from Manokotak—Carlson Kiunya—who died seal hunting. He was playing a piano like he always did during his earthly life. He was with an angel playing a golden harp. He told me they were getting ready for the great day of the feast of the Lamb of God. I saw the elders from back home [Manokotak]. They, too, were young—everyone was so young. I did not see anyone old. I thought, 'All these were old when they died on earth—how come they are young?' Jesus answered: 'Remember, I was 33 years old when I died on the cross and came up to heaven. All the people who accept me before they die—their souls will be young.' When the saved soul that was 100 years old dies and goes up to heaven, he'll be like Jesus. I guess I was the oldest guy up there. I never saw a gray hair up there—they all were young."

Abraham Meets His Deceased Relatives

"Again, I heard him say: 'Look.' Then He showed me my deceased relatives who were up there. He allowed me to see and talk with my late father, my grandparents, my great-grandparents, and my great-great-grandparents. Even though some of my relatives died before I was born, I knew them and they knew me. It was amazing! They were all young. My dad, Jesse, had his full set of hair and my grandpa had his full set of hair. At that time I was 42 years old and losing my hair. So when I get up there, I'll get it back!"

The Children in Heaven

"Again Jesus said: 'Atam!' I turned around and He showed me lots of little children—as far as my eyes could see—it looked like thousands of little children. They were all different nationalities. It seemed like they were floating around, moving up and down. I wondered what or who these were and before I could ask, He answered my thoughts and said, 'These are the children who were miscarried, aborted, stillborn, and the ones who died as infants. When their mothers accept me as their Savior, the children will recognize their mothers and they will be together for eternity.' You wouldn't want to come back to your body or this world once you see that place up there. I wanted to stay there forever."

"Then Jesus asked me, '**Do you want to see where the unsaved souls go?**'"

Chapter 5

HORRORS OF OUTER DARKNESS AND HELL

*"**B**efore I could answer His question, Jesus turned me around and off we went, away from the saved souls. He was standing right by me on my right side all the time. He never left me. Seems like we were on some sort of escalator going down—we were moving down fast—faster than walking. I looked at my legs and they were staying still but we were going away from the saved souls. I could feel the peace, joy, and love leaving me. It was terrifying!"*

~ABRAHAM GEORGE

THE TERRIBLE PLACE CALLED "OUTER DARKNESS"

"Before we reached that place of outer darkness I started smelling some awful smell. It was terrible—so terrible—a thousand times worse than anything I ever smelled on earth!

"When we got into that place it was pitch black—I could not see anything—it was like opening my eyes in liquid black tar. I never ever experienced blackness like that on earth. God is not there and there's no love inside that awful, stinky, pitch black place. It was cold-feeling—empty and dark.

"Then I heard people—it sounded like billions of people, but I couldn't see them. I heard gnashing of teeth, wailing, crying and souls screaming: 'I'm tired of being tormented… I'm thirsty… This is no place to be… Give me

another chance!' I heard my own Yup'ik language and seems like I heard all the languages of the earth. They all were begging for a second chance. On the third plea, Jesus would answer them. Everything was on three.

"I wondered who these were and why they were there. Jesus answered: 'These are the souls of the unprofitable servants and those that backslid. Jesus' voice sounded sad when he told them: 'While you were on earth I waited for you with outstretched arms to receive you, and I was ready to forgive you. But you didn't come to me. While you were on earth you never even believed the Word of God. You never even believed in me. You never had faith in me—you rejected me. While you were on earth you lived in earthly pleasure. Here's where you're going to be waiting until the judgment seat of Christ; and after that you'll be thrown into the lake of fire.'"

Author's Note: Abraham affirms that: "Outer darkness and hell are separate places—they're not joined." Outer darkness, as Abraham experienced and described it, is apparently some sort of stopover or waiting place of the lost dead on their dreadful journey to eternal judgment and final destiny in hell. This is the clear implication of Abraham's statement: "Here's where you're going to be waiting until the judgment seat of Christ, and after that you'll be thrown into the lake of fire."

THE "PITS" OF HELL

"Then from there we started going down toward the pits of hell. Jesus allowed me to see, hear, and smell, but He didn't allow me to feel what the lost souls were feeling. It's hard for me to describe hell. It was the total opposite of heaven. In all of hell there's no presence of God whatsoever. I could see the souls of people. So many, many souls are down there—millions upon millions I'd say. I heard countless souls loudly crying—crying in their own languages: 'This is no place to be... I'm tired of being tormented... Give me another chance.' If the whole state of Alaska hollered at the same time, it would be much louder than that! It was so terrible!

"While in hell, Jesus said: 'Look up!' and I looked up. He showed me more souls falling—it looked like black rain. He told me: 'These are mostly teenagers because they didn't honor their father and mother and were rebellious to their parents.' When they die they fall into hell because of their

44

sins. They are still falling even now!

"The souls in hell were all separated from one another. Each soul was in a separate pit and could not escape it. Each soul was alone—one soul in one pit. The pits looked something like beehive cells. There was fire upon them. The fire looked like molten lava or some kind of thick fire and it doesn't go out. The fire consumed that soul over and over nonstop. That place is dark but I could see the souls in the pits and they were covered with fire and worms. The fire was swirling around them like gas was thrown on them, but it didn't burn them up or the worms. They were covered with worms— completely covered. Their worms were from head on down to feet. The worms were in them. These vile worms were coming in and out from their mouths, eyes, noses, and ears. The worms did not burn and would not die."

THE THREE SOULS ABRAHAM MET IN HELL

"Then I heard these three souls who were in hell speaking in my own Yup'ik language."

THE HEDONISTIC[1] DRUNKARD

"The first soul Jesus caused me to meet was this poor soul who was a drunk and didn't have faith in Him. When his life was over he ended up in hell. There were worms all over him—worms came out from his nose, eyes, mouth, and ears. I heard him crying out in my own Yup'ik language: 'This is no place to be… I'm tired of being tormented… Give me another chance!' On the third plea Jesus answered him—everything was on three. Jesus answered: 'While you were on earth you never believed the Word of God and you lived in earthly pleasure. You did everything on earth contrary to what was written in the Word of God. You never believed in me. When you died you were drunk. This is where you're going to be until the great white throne judgment and then you'll be cast into the Lake of Fire.'"

THE CHURCH MINISTER

"And then Jesus showed me a second soul. That poor soul said, 'I was in church most of my life. I was a minister while on earth. How come I'm here? This is no place to be! I'm tired of being tormented I'm tired of being

---

1   Hedonist: a person whose life is devoted to the pursuit of pleasure and self-gratification. (Dictionary.com)

thirsty.' Then again on the third plea Jesus answered that poor soul and said: 'When you didn't care for that one least poor soul that nobody cared about; when you did that to him you did it to me. I was a stranger and you never accepted me. I was sick, you never came to me. I was hungry, you never fed me. I was in prison, you never came to me. When you didn't care for that one poor soul, you didn't care for me.' The one who thought he was a minister—at this time he is in hell. He's now suffering because he didn't have love for that one individual who was a child of God that nobody cared about."

Author's Note: Abraham told me that the minister's story was his most vivid and sobering memory of hell.

THE MAN WHO COMMITTED SUICIDE

"Then Jesus showed me a third poor soul, who took his own life. He was drunk at the time he killed himself. He thought he would escape the troubles of earth but when he took his own life he went straight to hell. Jesus told him: 'Before you were born I knew you. And I knew when your life would be taken. You took your own life—the one I gave you. You cheated your own life—you cut it short. When you were on earth you never even had faith in me. You never even read the Bible. This is where you're going to be until the great white throne judgment. In that you'll be judged and then you'll be thrown into the lake of fire. There you're going to be tormented forever [with] Satan and his angels.' Now at this moment, I'm afraid that poor soul who took his own life is in hell."

DEMONS IN HELL

"I saw demons moving around the pits—they looked like dark shadows. They circled the pits and as they passed by each, that soul would scream out in pain. Demons know Jesus and stay far from him. They can't stand to even come close to him."

CONCLUDING REMARKS

"My time in hell was enough for me to believe that there's outer darkness and there's hell, so I can tell His children those places are real! The Lord took me there so I could warn his children. 'Tell my children there's heaven and hell,' Jesus told me. 'This place is for the devil and his angels—not for my children. Tell my children: this is not their place; I don't want my children to end up in hell. Tell my children I am the way, the truth and the life. No man comes to the Father, but only by me.' Nobody would ever want to go down there!"

ABRAHAM ESCORTED BACK TO HEAVEN

"Then I thought in my mind, 'I don't want to be here! I don't want to be stuck in hell!' I wanted to get out of there as fast as I can. Jesus read my mind and said, 'I'm gonna take you back to heaven from the pit of hell.'"

Chapter 6

RETURN TO HEAVEN: FINAL COMMISSION & ANGELIC SEND-OFF

"*hen we were going up like on an elevator from that awful place. From the pits of hell, I felt we were going up—all of a sudden we were back in that bright and beautiful place and I smelled those beautiful smells again! I was so thankful—so relieved!*"

~ABRAHAM GEORGE

"*Jesus brought me back to where the saved souls are. I saw angels all over—there were so many different angels. They were wearing garments—seems like white fog was moving in and on their garments. I started hearing the angels glorifying God Almighty again, shouting: 'Glory, glory, glory!' and 'Holy, holy, holy!' Then everything in heaven glorified God Almighty. Again I saw all sorts of beautiful plants bursting their beautiful smells. I heard heavenly sounds—instruments, too. He allowed me to see my relatives again. I saw my late father, my grandparents, my great-grandma, my great-grandpa, my great-great grandpa. They were all so young. I saw many, many saved souls and all of them were young. I didn't see any old people at all. Jesus told me: 'All the people who accept me before they die, their souls will be young.'*"

~ABRAHAM GEORGE

ABRAHAM'S HEAVENLY COMMISSIONING

Just before being sent back to his body on Earth, Abraham was given a solemn commission from Jesus Himself:

> *"Tell my children there's heaven and hell. Hell is for the devil and his angels—not for my children. Tell my children: this is not their place; I don't want my children to end up in hell. Tell my children I am the way, the truth and the life, no man comes to the Father, but only by me. Tell my children I am coming soon, sooner than they think. I am at the door and looking at my Father and waiting for His command. When my Father says 'Go,' then I'm coming to get my children. The world is coming to an end—get ready!" Then Jesus said: "I'm going to bring you to places where you never even thought of going and you'll be persecuted the way I was persecuted. I'll be with you wherever you go."*

~ABRAHAM GEORGE

As he contemplated the magnitude of his assignment, his past lifestyle, the fact that he could barely speak English, and that he had never spoken publically before, Abraham came to a very logical conclusion —no one would ever believe him. It was an impossible task. He presented a reasonable and logical objection to Jesus: *"I told Jesus: 'No one will believe me.'"*

In response to Abraham's objections, Jesus gave Abraham several encouraging personal promises to strengthen and encourage him in preparation for the daunting task he was about to enter into. Abraham recalled the following promises.

Author's Note: From studying the transcript of Abraham's testimony along with the additional information gained from numerous interviews, it became apparent that Abraham had been given an essential three-part core message. The core message which Jesus gave Abraham was:

- *"Tell my children that I am the way and the truth and the life and no man comes unto the Father except through me.*

- *"Tell my children heaven and hell are real.*

- *"Tell my children I am coming soon-sooner than they think."*

This three-part message was repeated multiple times in various forms to Abraham while he was in heaven. To me it signified its paramount importance.

49

"Jesus answered me: 'When you speak, I'll be with you and my power will be with you. Everywhere you go, my Holy Spirit will be with you and the power of the Holy Spirit will be with you.' Again Jesus told me: 'You'll have friends that have my Spirit in them.' That's been happening everywhere I go."

Author's Note: I can confidently testify that Abraham has continued faithfully carrying out his assignment since he was released from the hospital on December 27, 2005, and generously includes the core messages whenever he retells his testimony.

As a result of receiving these encouraging promises, Abraham affirmed: "*This is why I can keep going and telling what I was told and don't worry.*"

DEPARTURE FROM HEAVEN AND CELESTIAL JOURNEY BACK TO EARTH

"*Then Jesus told me: 'I'm going to bring you back from heaven to your body.' I answered Him: 'I don't want to go back!' Then my late father, Jesse, appeared. He was in his 70's when he died—but he*

Angelic Send-off: Eileen found this artist's rendition on the internet. Abraham indicated that this was similar to what he saw as he was sent back to Earth from heaven.[1]

---

1 See Appendix for information regarding this artwork.

was young again! I wanted to stay there with him, but my dad told me sternly, 'Son, it's not your time—you've got to go back.' There were many, many angels all around us, too, and they were singing in my Yup'ik language, 'Silent Night, Holy Night.' It sounded like an enormous choir. That was the best and sweetest music I ever heard! It was awesome, awesome!

"Then Jesus started bringing me down to my body. He stayed at my right side on my way back and was talking to me all the way. Then Jesus showed me the whole earth—it was just like a blue marble. I was able to see it covered with clouds. It was real. The clouds were different—like glory clouds. I could see four big angels on earth's four corners. Then he showed me the whole state of Alaska. I saw small blue fires starting up in many places—here, there, here. I asked, 'What are these?' He said, 'I am pouring out my Holy Spirit upon all these places in these last days—there will be revival.' The Holy Spirit was the fire. I saw that I was coming to the earth and then, all of a sudden, I was in my body again."

~ABRAHAM GEORGE

Chapter 7
A CHRISTMAS DAY ARRIVAL ON EARTH

Abraham said: *"It was December 25th when I showed up in my body. I could still hear that awesome heavenly music of angels singing. The Lord was still with me. When I opened my eyes, even though it was daytime, everything looked dark compared to that place where I was. Then Jesus told me: 'Everywhere you go I'll be with you and when the time comes, after you're done with what I have told you to do, I'll get you.' When He gets me next time, I'll see Him face to face. Then He disappeared.*

"As the drugs left me, everything came back. I knew I had a wreck. I felt all the broken bones and lots of pain![1] Before, I was feeling no pain. Then I saw this light blue smoke circling my bed.

Author's Note: In a later interview, June told me that when Abraham told her about the blue smoke (which she herself could neither see nor smell) she went to the head nurse and reported what he had said. The head nurse told her to tell Abraham that "If the smoke got worse, they would call the fire department." June also spontaneously shared with me that of all the patients in her entire career, Abraham has had the most significant influence on her life.

"That cloud had a heavenly smell, like what I smelled in heaven. Every time when I breathed it in, I felt that beautiful blue smoke go right into my body—it felt like it had life in it. I felt tingling everywhere—from the top of my head to the soles of my feet. I asked that nurse named June, 'How come it's smoky? Is the hospital on fire?'"

---

1 *A detailed listing of Abraham's sever injuries can be found in Chapter 9.*

AN AMAZING THREE-DAY HEALING

Then Abraham said: *"Everything got healed during three days—Dec. 25th to Dec. 27th—in those 3 days that healing took place."* That claim statement was over the top for my Western influenced rational mind! I determined to put that astonishing claim on hold until I saw hard evidence to verify it.

Abraham continued relating his hospital experience: *"Then they called my family because they were going to unplug me from my life support. I guess that's what they did. On December 25th I showed up in my body. That was the day the doctors removed life support—my good lung had gotten pneumonia. Then our Lord Jesus put me back in my body and in three days I was healed! I came back to my body on December 25th, 2005. The doctors were puzzled, and said: 'How could this be?' This one doctor said, 'This is very puzzling.' They said, 'You're OK—you're well enough to walk.' Pretty amazing, all right!"*

A SECOND WITNESS TO ABRAHAM'S THREE-DAY HEALING

Melvin Andrew, one of the "Three Key Witnesses" in Chapter 10, provided the following corroborating information about Abraham's astonishing claimed three-day healing: *"I knew Abraham was going to die when I heard, on the public radio, his family's announcement that they were going to remove the life-support from him. That was December 23, 2005—I remember that day! Then, come December 25, I was surprised to hear an announcement on the public radio that Abraham George was awake and able to walk! The family thanked everyone who prayed for Abraham. I said in my mind: 'No way! He's supposed to be dead!'"*

Author's Note: The medical records neither confirm, nor deny, Abraham's three-day healing claim. I have accepted it as genuine for the following three reasons:

- *First, because of the credibility of Melvin Andrew's testimony.*
- *Second, because I am persuaded that no one could possibly know better than Abraham himself regarding his own body's condition.*
- *Third, because of Abraham's consistent, proven integrity. In the several years that I've know him, I have asked him multitudes of questions many times and his story has never changed.*

ABRAHAM'S DEPARTURE FROM HOSPITAL

On December 27, 2005, Abraham was healed sufficiently to walk out the door of the Alaska Native Medical Center on his own two feet (with the aid of crutches) to begin his new life—*a life that no one could ever have imagined!* Abraham George had an amazing and an urgent message to convey and he began telling it immediately—he said: *"Nothing held me back!"*

Chapter 8
A SPREADING FLAME: SPIRITUAL REVIVAL HITS ALASKA

"*Then Jesus showed me the whole state of Alaska. He showed me little fires coming out in the small places. 'What is this,' I asked? He answered: 'He's pouring out His Holy Spirit upon all these places in these last days. Everywhere you go, my Holy Spirit will be with you and my power will be with you. There will be revival.'*"

~ABRAHAM GEORGE
VISION OF ALASKA WHILE TRAVELING FROM HEAVEN BACK TO EARTH

Abraham's celestial experience and commission was so real and so compelling that as soon as he was physically able, he urgently began telling others about it—first to hospital staff, then his family and hospital visitors. Abraham described the intensity of his mindset when he first came back as: "*Nothing held me back! Right away I told that nurse, June, that was with me and those doctors. I told the visitors that came and visited me from all over Alaska.*" Abraham's mother, Mary, who had made daily visits to pray for her son while he was comatose, along with her husband (Ipli's stepfather), were the first to believe Abraham's story. His mother stated:

> "*He was in a coma a long time. After he woke up we went to see him and he said he had experienced hell and heaven. He captured both of us.*"
>
> ~MARY KANULIE (*FORMERLY MARY GEORGE*)

Mary (George) Kanulie, Ipli's mother.

After Abraham's release from the hospital on December 27, 2005, he continued receiving outpatient physical therapy for about ten days to help restore his ability to walk normally. Ipli's mother reported: *"At the hospital chapel Abraham was sharing his testimony. He stayed with us when he left the hospital."* News of Abraham's amazing experience soon began circulating among Anchorage churches and he started accepting invitations to tell his story at several. *"I went to churches in Anchorage and gave my testimony. I did that right away."* This accelerated public awareness.

ABRAHAM RETURNS TO MANOKOTAK

On the morning of January 7, 2006, Abraham boarded a commuter plane at the Anchorage airport and was headed back home to Manokotak. Little did Abraham realize that he was carrying within himself the seed of Holy Spirit revival which would soon break out in Manokotak and then would spread like a fire to the villages of Western Alaska and beyond.

As soon as Abraham arrived back in Manokotak, *"People started greeting him at his house and right away he started talking about his encounters with heaven and hell"* (Ken Nukwuk). Abraham said: *"I told many people."* His testimony instantly became the leading topic of discussion in the village and on the VHF household radio network and remained in first place for the next several weeks.

Then it was announced on the radio that Abraham was planning to tell his whole story the following Sunday night, January 15th, 2006, at the church—the only one in the village. That evening the church building was packed—people were even standing in the aisles. Sally Nukwak, a neighbor of Abraham and a village health aide, was present and reported: *"The church was packed to hear his testimony."* The atmosphere

56

was electric with excitement and curiosity, as the nefarious town drunk slowly made his way to the podium, nursing a slight limp—the room grew dead silent. Then Abraham picked up the microphone, and began boldly and fervently telling his spectacular story of God, the glory of heaven and the terrifying horrors of outer darkness and hell. At the conclusion of his moving message, more than an hour later, he ended his impassioned speech by throwing out a challenge for all the doubters in the crowd: *"If this is from God, it will last. If not, it will go away."*

His fellow villagers were astounded by Abraham's graphic description of his celestial sights and experiences. They were all the more impressed by the authoritative manner of his presentation. Some thought that it didn't even sound like the Abraham they had known.

At the conclusion of Abraham's speech an open invitation was extended for any who desired to be prayed for. Many responded. Abraham and other leaders laid their hands on and prayed for them. Several of those prayed for fell to the floor as though struck by lightning![1] Nothing like this had ever before occurred in Manokotak. When the prayer time was finished, the cold floor at the front of the little church was strewn with warm bodies—some writhing, some crying, some laughing—it was astonishing. The **power** which Abraham had been promised by Jesus while in heaven was beginning to be released in his home village of Manokotak. The humble and little-known village of Manokotak would never be the same, for it was chosen to be the launch site for spiritual revival in Alaska.

A SURPRISE MESSENGER ARRIVES IN MANOKOTAK WITH A MESSAGE FROM GOD FOR ABRAHAM

The week following that historic meeting, an unscheduled plane touched down on Manokotak's gravel airstrip. The lone passenger disembarked from the plane. His name was Glen Moses, a man Abraham vaguely knew from his past. The unexpected visitor had chartered that plane from Bethel for the sole purpose of delivering an urgent personal message to

---

1   *See pgs. 60-61 for an explanation of these spiritual manifestations, under the subheading* SPIRITUAL FEASTS AND SIGNS OF REVIVAL.

Abraham, which he claimed to have received directly from God. His message was short and stern—admonishing Abraham to: *"not give up telling his children and to tell it the way He showed you everything"* (Glen Moses, as related by Abraham George). Abraham received that message as authentic and took it to heart. He understood its meaning as a heaven-sent admonition to not enhance or change anything from his experiences and the three-part message he had been entrusted with. He must just keep on telling it, which he has faithfully done.

Author's Note: Question to ponder: How sure do you think Glen Moses was— regarding the authenticity and importance of his message—for him to have spent a minimum of $600 and two days of his life just to deliver it to Abraham?

For Abraham, Glen's message was a timely and refreshing word of encouragement for he had been wrestling with bouts of self-doubt and simultaneously discouragement from the unrelenting harassment of a handful of village skeptics and critics—the foremost and most painful of which was his own wife, Eileen. Melvin Andrew commented about her hurtful harassment: *"Eileen would get on the village VHF radio network and publicly castigate Abraham, calling him a liar, a hypocrite, a devil, and openly spoke of his shameful past."* Needless to say, Abraham didn't come home to a warm, loving, and understanding wife. She would not soon forget the painful abuse he had inflicted upon her over the previous 25 years. Whenever she heard him tell his story it provoked her to anger. She **utterly** rejected it, considering it ridiculous.

A Spreading Flame:
Miracles Break Out in Manokotak

Abraham's bold declaration of his testimony at the Manokotak church turned out to be a landmark event for the village of Manokotak and for Abraham. Several of the people Abraham had prayed for soon experienced profound and verifiable healings. With the aid of the VHF radio network, the sensational news of healing miracles literally exploded throughout the village. Abraham's cell phone began ringing constantly and the flow of visitors to his front door quickly multiplied. Some came with questions, but most were desperately wanting prayer for themselves or for ailing relatives. Melvin Andrew spoke of this unusual occurrence saying: *"Abraham still visits those in need of prayer and many still visit him at his home asking for prayer. Abraham's door is always open to anyone."* The people coming for prayer snowballed. The more people Ipli prayed for, the more healings there were, which in turn resulted in even **more** people coming to his door for prayer. When Abraham was asked for his estimate of the number of miraculous healings he had witnessed in Manokotak, he responded: *"There are so many I can't keep track of it."*

In this way, Abraham was thrust into his prayer healing ministry. Melvin Andrew shared his eyewitness observations of this never-before-seen phenomena stating: *"Abraham George prayed for the sick and they were healed. Abraham George prayed for the hurting and they became whole. Abraham George prayed for many to believe and many accepted Christ as their personal Lord and savior."*

Reports soon reached Moravian Bishop, "Doc" Nicholson, in Anchorage who reported: *"I heard—astonishingly— how this guy was now winning souls for the kingdom. It sounded like the force of his personality and life-change was creating great religious fervor in the village of Manokotak. I have heard of many young people in Manokotak turning their lives over to Christ—folks who would never entertain going to church—now filling the Moravian Church and having home Bible studies. This struck me as unusual. It sounded like Manokotak was experiencing revival."*

The first "small flame" of revival which Abraham had seen in his vision while returning from heaven, had been ignited—in Manokotak. Word of it spread like a wildfire throughout Western Alaska. Abraham began receiving invitations from neighboring villages to come and share his testimony in person.

A SPREADING FLAME: THE UNIQUE ALASKAN "SPIRITUAL FEAST" MOVEMENT

In October 2006 a group of "spiritually on-fire" young people, led by Rachel Nelson in the village of Kwigillingok in Southwestern Alaska, were inspired to initiate a spiritual event which they called a "Spiritual Feast." The designation "Spiritual Feast" was soon adopted to describe the new grassroots spiritual revival movement in the villages of Southwestern Alaska. The Kwigillingok event became the prototype and inspiration for many future Spiritual Feasts.

Abraham was invited to present his testimony at the Kwigillingok "Spiritual Feast." This was his first speaking engagement out of Manokotak. Ipli, along with his band of six "on-fire disciples" from Manokotak, made their first team mission trip there. That trip also marked the beginning of Abraham's "Spiritual Feast" ministry. Sally Nukwak, commented about this, saying: *"He started traveling to villages soon after [the landmark Manokotak church service] and a lot of villages were hungry to hear his testimony. The following Spiritual Feasts took place each year and he'd speak and people young and old would commit their lives to Christ."* It is believed that Kwigillingok was the second "small revival fire" to ignite, which Abraham had seen in his vision.

WHAT IS A "SPIRITUAL FEAST"?

A Spiritual Feast is an informal gathering of primarily indigenous Alaskans from a variety of villages. There is no formal program or liturgy—the intent being to allow the Holy Spirit to lead as much as possible through chosen lay leaders. The purpose of the Spiritual Feast is threefold: to praise and worship God, to seek a personal transformational "touch" by the Holy Spirit and to enjoy good old-fashioned Christian fellowship and feasting. Activities of the spiritual feast include some or all of the following: lots of joyful and rousing singing (mostly older gospel hymns typically with a light country-western flair); solos, duets, or larger groups; personal testimonies; Bible readings and classes; sermons; prayer and ministry times; fellowship and feasting. It is a happy, joyful time of spontaneous worship and praise.

SPIRITUAL FEASTS AND SIGNS OF REVIVAL

During the ministry time, which normally occurs as the final event of the evening service, leaders lay their hands on those desiring prayer. This typically results in a wide range of unusual and often strange responses to the power of the Holy Spirit. The manifestations may include some or all of the following: people falling to the floor (the experience feels like all the strength in your legs instantly leaves), uncontrollable and contagious laughter, crying or sobbing, joyful dancing with hands uplifted and shouting praises. These prayer ministry times have proven effective to produce powerful life transformations—especially when Abraham George is ministering. Bishop Nicholson related his observations while attending the 2008 Manokotak Spiritual Feast: *"Every spiritual gift of the Holy Spirit seemed to be in operation at the Feast. This was evident through specific manifestations of healing; people being set free from sin and addictions; repentance, forgiveness—the aisle was full of marriage partners confessing faults and desiring marriage renewal. Tears of forgiveness and joy were everywhere. This is a new manifestation of God's grace and freedom never before evident in the Moravian Churches in Alaska."*

ANOTHER TYPE OF FEAST

Rachel Nelson, who is the person credited as the originator of the first Spiritual Feast in Kwigillingok, shared her personal definition of this event as follows: *"The Spiritual Feast is like a potluck—people come and bring different kinds of food—main dishes and dessert. People come in from different churches to share, sing, and have a feast together."* A potluck feast has, from its inception, been an important and enjoyable aspect of these gatherings. Participants feast on a rich array of native foods served smorgasbord style. Native entrée selections typically include some or all of the following: dried whitefish; dried, smoked, pickled, and baked salmon; pickled herring; "muktuk" (raw whale blubber still attached to the 3/8 inch thick gray leathery hide); roasted or fermented walrus meat; roast moose and caribou; raw or roasted beluga whale; boiled sea duck; fresh and fermented seal oil, which is the universal Eskimo condiment and is used primarily as a gourmet spread or dipping sauce for nearly anything or everything (it tastes like "fishy" olive oil); and there is always the all-time favorite dessert—Eskimo ice cream, called "akutaq," which is a concoction of hand-picked wild berries, sugar, and Crisco. Fortunately, there is also normally a limited selection of "gussok"(white man) food—featuring white bread, boiled rice; chicken, or ham. I have personally sampled all of the above (with the exception of fermented walrus meat) and my tongue definitely prefers good ol' "gussok" food.

ABRAHAM GEORGE
AND THE SPIRITUAL FEAST MOVEMENT

Abraham has never laid claim to being the originator nor the one responsible for advancing the Spiritual Feast movement. The hard facts, however, clearly indicate that it would be nearly impossible to explain its rapid and widespread growth apart from his involvement and strong influence. The following facts support this claim:

First, the Spiritual Feast movement began *after* Abraham had his profound out-of-body experience in 2005, and *after* he was used to spark the revival in Manokotak.

Second, several reputable and knowledgeable leaders have expressed their recognition of Abraham's vital role with the Spiritual Feast. Bishop Nelson (one of the leaders of the Alaska Moravian church), stated: *"What is happening started from one man only... It started and is based upon his personal testimony."* Bishop Nicholson (another of the Moravian leaders) said: *"Certainly it may have taken one man to spark an interest in God's power and glory... Manokotak had their own outpouring and I believe Abraham George was the sparkplug."* Melvin Andrew went on record saying: *"Abraham George certainly did play an important role in God's scheme of things in reference to the Spiritual Feast."*

Third, Abraham presented his testimony at the first-ever Spiritual Feast in Kwigillingok and has done so at nearly every other Spiritual Feast.

> *"Abraham George went to Kwigillingok and gave his testimony."*
> ~MELVIN ANDREW

Fourth, Abraham has been a significant attraction for the Spiritual Feasts he attends, for virtually every villager has wanted to meet him in person to hear his testimony firsthand or to be prayed for by him:

62

"A lot of villages were hungry to hear his testimony."

~SALLY NUKWAK

Fifth, Manokotak conducted the second Spiritual Feast in 2007 and has continued holding one annually ever since. *"Spiritual Feasts took place each year [after 2007]"* (Sally Nukwak). The Manokotak leadership of the Spiritual Feast movement has been an ongoing stimulus and inspiration for other villages to also continue holding them. This connection was recognized and acknowledged by Bishop Nicholson stating: *"The Spiritual Feast roots as a renewal movement began in Kwigillingok and flowered in Manokotak. The Manokotak Moravian Church young people's leadership have been at the forefront of renewal."*

The above facts clearly establish the fact that Abraham George has truly been an integral and vital factor in the development and progress of the Spiritual Feast movement. It has become yet another significant way he is being used to fan the flame of revival in Alaska.

A SPREADING FLAME:
ABRAHAM TURNED "TRAVELING EVANGELIST"

"Jesus told me: 'I'm going to bring you back from heaven to your body and I'm going to bring you places where you never even thought of going.'"

~ABRAHAM GEORGE

Abraham was thus predestined to undergo one more radical life change. He was about to don the mantle of a traveling evangelist. Abraham said: *"I already knew that I was to tell the story because He told me He was going to send me to places."*

Abraham's travels prior to 2005 were limited primarily to the 20-mile run to Dillingham to buy his booze or other things hard to find in Manokotak. And of course, there were also the numerous state-financed trips to jail in Anchorage. Since his quick healing and release from the Anchorage hospital, Abraham's travels have expanded greatly. Abraham has logged thousands of ministry miles—by small plane, boat, snowmobile, automobile and on foot—retelling his story.

"Now I'm traveling for His will, he's taking care of everything while I'm traveling."

~ABRAHAM GEORGE

Henry Shavings Jr., a long-time resident of Manokotak and one of Abraham's earliest Manokotak disciples and traveling companions, provided the following impressive report of Abraham's first multi-village evangelistic tour which Henry and eight others participated in: *"The most significant travels I had with Ipli was when we traveled to Chevak, Hooper Bay, and Scammon Bay—nine of us on a plane! There were so many conversions that we couldn't keep count."* (Abraham remarked that in each of these three villages the gymnasiums were "packed with people".) *"During all our travels [which took place between 2006 and 2010], I would estimate there were at the very least 1700-plus that gave their hearts to the Lord."*

In the winter of 2010 he completed a 30-day, 500-mile marathon sno-go trip, making three-day stopovers in 10 different villages. Reporting on the results of that trip, Abraham said: *"Countless souls accepted Jesus and many got healed... and so many relatives got saved."*

Author's Note: In missions, especially in the remote native villages of Alaska, the scenario is highly unusual, as any missionary would attest. This openness to the Spirit and the gospel is a telling witness to the effectiveness and authenticity of Abraham's ministry, for his only advertisement and promotion has been word-of-mouth.

Bishop Nicholson recognized this unusual phenomenon and said: "Villages that have been essentially closed to the gospel are opening up en masse before this man of God."

It is important to understand regarding Abraham's mission travels that they have all been by **invitation only** and most of the requests have also included payment of his travel expenses. Melvin Andrew commented on this unusual phenomenon: *"Abraham is now welcomed in other communities, churches, and places to share his testimony. He is constantly traveling to other villages and is being requested to speak in their places of worship."*

Abraham has coursed the native villages of Alaska from the Inupiaq whaling village of Barrow on the Arctic Ocean, to the island village of Sitka, on the rain-forested coast of the Southeast Panhandle (home of the Haida, Tsimshian, and Tlingit tribes), 1,100 miles away. Abraham's ministry has, without persuasion or conflict, penetrated every **cultural, tribal, denominational, and racial barrier** isolating Alaska's villages. He has shared his testimony in over **78** Alaskan villages including Alaska's four major population centers—Anchorage, Wasilla, Juneau, and Fairbanks.

Author, Abraham, & Eileen en route to Kiana, AK

HEALING MIRACLES FAN THE FLAME

"Everywhere when we start praying for the people, the healing takes place. There are too many names and too many healed that I don't keep track of it."

~ABRAHAM GEORGE

When Melvin Andrew was asked about the number of healing miracles he had personally witnessed, he answered: *"Too many to name!"*

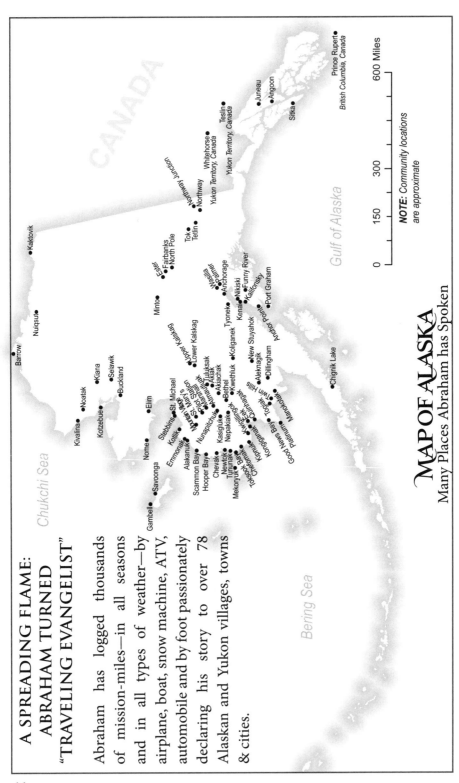

A SPREADING FLAME: ABRAHAM TURNED "TRAVELING EVANGELIST"

Abraham has logged thousands of mission-miles—in all seasons and in all types of weather—by airplane, boat, snow machine, ATV, automobile and by foot passionately declaring his story to over 78 Alaskan and Yukon villages, towns & cities.

MAP OF ALASKA
Many Places Abraham has Spoken

CANADA

Chukchi Sea

Bering Sea

Gulf of Alaska

NOTE: Community locations are approximate

0   150   300   600 Miles

Barrow
Kaktovik
Nuiqsut
Kiana
Noatak
Selawik
Buckland
Kivalina
Kotzebue
Elim
Nome
Gambell
Savoonga
Minto
Ester
Fairbanks
North Pole
Tok
Teller
Northway Junction
Northway
Yukon Territory, Canada
Whitehorse
Yukon Territory, Canada
Teslin
Juneau
Angoon
Sitka
Prince Rupert
British Columbia, Canada

Wasilla
Palmer
Anchorage
Nikiski
Funny River
Kenai
Kalifonsky
Anchor Point
Port Graham

Stebbins
St. Michael
Kotlik
Mountain Village
St. Mary's
Pilot Station
Marshall
Upper Kalskag
Lower Kalskag
Tuluksak
Akiak
Akiachak
Tyonek
Aniak
Kwethluk
Koliganek
New Stuyahok
Alakanuk
Scammon Bay
Hooper Bay
Emmonak
Nunapitchuk
Bethel
Kasigluk
Chevak
Newtok
Tununak
Nightmute
Toksook Bay
Mekoryuk
Chefornak
Kipnuk
Kongiganak
Kwigillingok
Good News Bay
Manokotak
Twin Hills
Togiak
Aleknagik
Dillingham
Chignik Lake

2011: Abraham in Sitka, on a mission trip to Juneau and Angoon, Alaska.

Manifestations of the supernatural instantly ignited a firestorm of interest in Abraham's ministry. Miracles, more than anything else, have been the wind fanning the flame of revival in Alaska.

When it comes to credible personal testimonies of healings, the problem has not been in finding them, but rather in selecting which to include. In the acquisition of the details of miracles however, there have been two recurring cultural challenges to work through. The first was clearly stated by Abraham himself: *"Us Eskimos don't like questions."* (Especially from prying "gussoks" like me.) I boldly responded to him: *"Well, you'll just have to get over it, because if you don't answer my questions, you'll be answering the same questions thousands of times in the future."* There also seems to be a lingering suspicion and distrust toward gussoks (white folks), among natives in general, probably due to horrendous past abuses.[2] Because of these factors, extracting details from Abraham and the many other Native Alaskans quoted in this book has, at times, been difficult.

Author's Note: Instances of such abuses include the loss of cultural identity and integrity through removing native children from their homes and villages to government boarding schools and the forced abandonment of native languages.

No man can heal the pain and abuse of the past, but representing, and on behalf of all the gussok abuses of the past upon First Nation peoples, I apologize and ask forgiveness.

A second challenge has been that Abraham, and most other indigenous people, have been raised in a culture of oral tradition. Thus Abraham has never kept written records of any of the multitudes of unusual or supernatural events which have characterized his ministry from its beginning. Bishop Nicholson became aware of this and commented: *"I know one thing—[Abraham] doesn't keep track of how many souls he's won. I had to hear from a secondary source that over 700 people came to know the Lord on that one trip. One of the individuals that followed him up there kept track."*

Abraham's habit of not keeping count is also possibly due to his aversion

---

2   *It is beyond the scope of this book to go into depth regarding this crucial issue. For interested readers, please see the Resources section after the Appendix for links to information on "Alaska Natives' Loss of Social & Cultural Integrity".*

to receiving personal credit for any of the good and sensational things that have taken place in his ministry. All this to say—it has made the procurement of specific details challenging.

PERSONAL HEALING TESTIMONIES

The following testimonies are only a small sampling of the witnesses to the effects of the powerful wind that has been an integral part of Abraham's ministry.

TOGIAK, ALASKA

"When I heard Ipli testify in Togiak, he was really glowing! Something was around him—he was so clean... A few accepted and got saved...some changed... Some got healed of sickness. I knew he was telling the truth."
~MOSES AYOJIAK
TOGIAK, ALASKA

Moses, along with his wife, later became committed members in Abraham's ministry traveling team.

Moses Ayojiak

CHEVAK, ALASKA

John & Teresa Pingayak, Abraham's ministry travelling compainions

"On December 8, 2008, Abraham George traveled to Chevak with people from Manokotak. Before the [Spiritual Feast] gathering and testimony of Ipli, he and Paul Jenkins blessed olive oil for anointing. And before we went to the community hall, my daughter's baby fell from my high bed to the iron frame of the bed. There was a black-and-blue mark the size of a

golf ball. I applied the anointing oil on the affected area and went up to listen to the testimony of Ipli. Inside the community hall people gathered in multitudes to listen to the testimony of heaven and hell. After about 30 minutes, my daughter Liana came with the baby and said, 'Look Dad—it's gone!' The wound was completely gone."

~JOHN PINGAYAQ
LIFETIME RESIDENT OF CHEVAK

DILLINGHAM, ALASKA

"[Abraham] talks to a lot of people and prays for them. A lot of people have changed and have become new people. Before [Abraham prayed for me], I didn't want to be outside my house and now I'm very happy—always positive and living for the Lord."

"After Abraham prayed for my friend, Patsy Nelson, she went from having rheumatoid arthritis and not wanting to do anything—to hunting, fishing, cooking, berry picking—a whole different person. Before she accepted God in her life, she could not get up from bed. Now she has a very positive outlook on life."

"My [at the time] fiancé, Kevin Tennyson, was diagnosed with two [double] pneumonias and we couldn't figure out why. He kept coughing and was struggling to breathe. He was on four or five medications and steroids. All this fall he's been in that bad condition. After getting prayed for at my house by Ipli on Saturday, March 5th, he went from being bed-ridden to two hours later he got up and was able to chop wood and fix my entryway and went outside without being short of breath. He was crying tears of happiness because God healed him".

~SIRENA TENNYSON

ST. MICHAEL, ALASKA

The testimony of Priscilla Levi, a mother of five children from Saint Michael, Alaska (172 miles Southeast of Nome), is one of the most profound healing testimonies that I have heard and warrants giving more details. I had heard about Priscilla's healing miracle from several reputable sources, but in October, 2008 I finally met her in Manokotak and interviewed her in person. The following report is based on that interview.

Priscilla Levi's story begins with a serious four-wheeler (ATV) accident which occurred while she was traveling on an icy road to a neighboring village. The shoulders of the road were steep and covered with large boulders. Here is Priscilla's account of that accident and its aftermath.

Priscilla Levi

"I was traveling by Honda to the next village. On the way there, I slid off the road—there were big boulders. I landed hard and heard a crunch and I hit my head. When I got checked at the clinic, I was told that I cracked my collarbone, fractured my right shoulder blade, and tore muscles in my neck and back. I couldn't even put my head down or back; I couldn't lift my arm without pain. Every time I moved my arm I heard crunches. In the meantime, eight months passed and I was still in pain when I went to be prayed for by Abraham at the gymnasium."

~Priscilla Levi

"The organizers of the Saint Michael's Spiritual Feast had reserved the high school auditorium for the special occasion. Nearly everyone in the village was packed into the gymnasium that evening to hear Abraham—everyone except Priscilla Levi. At the conclusion of Abraham's testimony and hands-on prayer ministry, nearly every soul present responded to the gospel invitation— I would guess that 200 made decisions for Christ and many received healings."

~Sally Teluk
Eek, Alaska

Regarding the Saint Michael meeting, Abraham reported: *"When I finished praying for the people, the gym floor was nearly covered with people [laid out]."*

Though Priscilla had previously heard about the community-wide event planned for Abraham's visit, she decided not to attend and instead, to make a grocery run to the neighboring village of Stebbins, a few miles away. Priscilla arrived back home at St. Michael from Stebbins at about the same time the Spiritual Feast was ending.

Priscilla continues her story: *"When I got back, my kids were telling me I needed to go see this man."* Priscilla was resisting the idea, saying it was too late and the meeting was over. However, her oldest daughter persisted. *"My daughter kept saying, 'No, Mom, you need to go!' They were almost dragging me! So I thought that if he was this awesome, I might as well go."*

Author's Note: Doesn't it just make you wonder what Priscilla's daughters had seen and heard at the meeting?

Fortunately for Priscilla, her daughter's persistence prevailed and she relented and went with her oldest daughter to the gymnasium. When they arrived at the village gymnasium the ministry time was already over. Upon entering, Priscilla was shocked to see dozens of her friends and neighbors scattered willy-nilly all over the gym floor—some laughing, some crying, and some ghostly still. She felt awkward, embarrassed and fearful as she carefully maneuvered her way through the strewn bodies to present herself to Abraham, the man of God, to ask him to pray for her physical healing. Here's what happened next:

"While he was praying for me, I felt a presence behind me and a bright light, like from a giant flashlight, shone on me and Abraham. Then I got weak and I almost fell to the floor. There were five other people that had their hands on me and were holding me up. Abraham kept praying. I felt hot. Then I and the people that were standing around me heard my bones cracking and noises like popping. Then I felt my back go straight and I stood up straight [for

the first time in eight months]. I felt no more pain. I said 'I feel no more pain! I feel better!' I thank God that he was sent [our] way to help us believe."

~PRISCILLA LEVI

NAPAKIAK, ALASKA

In 2009, when Abraham and his ministry team arrived in the village of Napakiak, Alaska, they were immediately asked by those who met them at the airport to come to the home of Annie Nelson, an elderly woman, to pray for her healing, as she had been sick and bedridden for two weeks. Mrs. Nelson described her condition as: *"in extreme pain constantly, lack of sleep, no appetite. I couldn't get up from bed, go to the bathroom, walk, or go to eat—medications did not help me, only little bit."* Then, as Abraham began anointing her with oil and praying, a mysterious mist, like fog, suddenly appeared in the room. Annie continued: *"I felt tingling from his hand, a sense of calm and quiet and peace. I started getting up on my own to do my house chores and was able to skin-sew again."* Eileen George was present and witnessed the strange mist and the healing, and shared what impressed her the most: *"Annie jumped out of bed and began running around the room, full of joy like a little girl!"*

PILOT STATION, ALASKA

"Before Abraham George was sent by God to the Yukon River, my life was a terrible mess. I was full of hatred and was an unloving father and husband. I nearly lost my family and also nearly took my own life. Abraham George prayed for me on October 18, 2007, during the Spiritual Feast in Manokotak and suddenly I saw a blackness come out of me and a bright light shone into me. I soon realized that I was not the same. I am now an evangelist for Jesus Christ and Minister on the Yukon River."

Michael Tinker at the 2007 Manokotak Spiritual Feast

~MICHAEL TINKER
ITINERANT EVANGELIST, PILOT STATION, ALASKA

73

TOKSOOK BAY, ALASKA

When Abraham and his team arrived in the western Alaska village of Toksook Bay, they learned that the local church, which was mostly Catholic, had been chronically splintered into factions. Felix Lincoln, a long-time resident and one of the members of that splintered church, was present when Abraham ministered there. Felix later reported on the outcome of that meeting:

> *"I would like to report that as a result of Abraham George's visit and ministry, the Toksook Bay Fellowship is reunited in one body and one Spirit. All the people that were at the gathering came forward to be prayed for. The next day there was true healing and forgiveness amongst the congregation. Now we are reunited like there was no division at all."*

~FELIX LINCOLN
TOKSOOK BAY, ALASKA

ANCHORAGE, ALASKA

BEYOND THE GRAVE

HEAR THE AMAZING ACCOUNT OF THIS MAN'S EXPERIENCE OF
DEATH AND HIS JOURNEY TO HEAVEN AND HELL AND BACK!

ABRAHAM GEORGE

In 2005, this Yup'ik Eskimo, had a fatal snow-machine accident. He then had an amazing "out-of-body" experience with Jesus Christ and was transformed from a hard-core drug addict and alcoholic to an on-fire Evangelist. He has been traveling and telling his experience ever since. Hundreds of souls have received salvation and many miraculous physical healings have occurred. This is your invitation to hear his story.

WHEN? FEBRUARY 24TH TWO SERVICES: 10:00 AM AND 6:30 PM

WHERE? SKYLINE CHURCH ON DOWLING, A BLOCK WEST OF LAKE OTIS
(THE OLD DMV BUILDING)

FREE! ADMISSION   COME EARLY!   SEATING IS LIMITED!

*Abraham George: Skyline Church
Meeting Poster, 2013*

Abraham comes to Anchorage fairly often nowadays, due to the fact that his mother and two daughters live there. When in Anchorage, he typically receives several phone calls a day from people in outlying villages, requesting him to go and pray for their hospitalized family and relatives. On an average day in Anchorage, Abraham is requested to make from one to several hospital visits. The following testimonies are a small sampling of reported results of this ministry.

74

"My husband [Leonard] had a stroke from a brain aneurysm. Ipli came [to ANMC—Alaska Native Medical Center, Anchorage] and prayed for him. The next day he got an MRI and he was better! He came home shortly after that."

~TERESA OLRUN
ABRAHAM'S AUNT, ANCHORAGE

"My mother was in the hospital in Anchorage [ANMC] for cancer last year. Abraham came to pray for her and when he was touching her with oil for healing she felt healing all the way down from her head to her feet. She really felt the power of God and her and my father smelled the aroma of heaven in the room. At her checkup she had no cancer. Her name is Pauline Andrew. She is still cancer-free."

~ARLENE FRANKLIN
MANOKOTAK

"I was hospitalized for a week in Dillingham for pneumonia symptoms and after that I got sicker and sicker so they sent me to a specialist in Anchorage [ANMC]. My symptoms were: coughing nonstop for months, trouble with breathing, dizziness, all kinds of stuff. They took x-rays that showed that I had pneumonia and asthma and black spots in my lower lungs.

"Ipli prayed for me, and 'Doc' William [also prayed later that day]. When they were praying I felt like electricity going from my head to my chest all the way through my body to my feet and it lasted about a minute. After I was prayed for... the coughing, the lung problems—everything went away—I was healed! The next day I had an appointment with my doctor. She checked me and my lungs and the usual stuff they do. She asked how I felt and I said, 'Good!' She looked at me and said, 'I got the test results back from the hospitals I sent you to and this perplexed me. I don't know how this happened, but the symptoms that you had when you first came in are gone! You look so good—what happened to you?' I told her I got prayed for and got healed and she said, 'Wow, you're weird.'"

~BLINN DULL
DILLINGHAM, ALASKA

An Extraordinary Cell Phone Ministry

Abraham's cell phone began ringing off the hook as soon as the news got out about the explosion of numerous miraculous healings in Manokotak. That began another phase of Abraham's outreach ministry. Since that early beginning in 2006, Ipli has literally been on his cell phone several hours a day. Admittedly, just hanging all day on a cell phone is nothing impressive in itself, but it is the **content and purpose** of his calls which I have found extremely unusual. Nearly all of his calls are **received calls**. They come primarily from complete strangers in villages all over Alaska, they come from people from a wide variety of denominational and tribal backgrounds. The common denominator is that they are people in desperate need and are requesting prayer.

Here is a man—Abraham—without credentials, theological or counseling training, and essentially biblically illiterate. Yet, in spite of his lack, he is still earnestly sought after nearly every day for counsel and prayer. This leaves one to wonder—what is the driving force of these calls? The conclusion I have come to is simply this: **when Abraham prays, people get answers**.

Bethel Prison Revival by DVD and Cell Phone

Because of Abraham's felony record, he has been barred from entering any of Alaska's state prisons. There is one prison, however—the Yukon Kuskokwim, in Bethel, Alaska—where Abraham has still had a huge impact on the inmates, in spite of never having set foot in the facility. This has been accomplished through the use of only his cell phone and a low quality DVD of his testimony, which is available for inmates to view in the prison library.

I spoke with the two pastoral volunteers who minister weekly in the YKCC facility and they reported being aware of the impact that Abraham's testimony had been having on many inmates. I also learned from them that an incredible 60% of YKCC inmates regularly participate in Bible studies and worship services. Abraham has received countless phone calls and personal letters from YKCC inmates, requesting prayers and counsel. Below are excerpts from four of many letters which verify this phenomena.

September 28, 2009—*"Since I came into Bethel prison I started to spread the testimony of brother Abraham George. The word spread immediately. There's been a lot of Holy Spirit activity among the inmates... It was amazing how the Holy Spirit was touching the inmates and other prisoners in the dorms. Another inmate was touched by the Holy Spirit and he stated that he will ask forgiveness from everyone that he has hurt. When he left prison he took his Bible with him home. On another day I started to mention the testimony of Abraham George and pass his cell number around to inmates and, wow! The presence of the Holy Spirit was all over the building. The presence was so strong we kept on praying and a lot of people said they wanted to change their lives and wanted to live without troubles anymore and don't want to come back here again. Since I've been spreading the word and Brother Abraham's cell number a lot of people are realizing and understanding who Jesus really is. There's a lot going on here— praise the Lord!"*

~A.M., INMATE AT YKCC

October 6, 2009—*"Dear Abraham George, I'm writing to you from prison in Bethel. I am requesting your prayers for my parents and family. Also please pray for me. I'm sorry I missed hearing your testimony when you were in Marshall—I was moose hunting."*

~L.E. SR., INMATE AT YKCC

September 11, 2009—*"Hello brother Abe, After you prayed for me (by cell phone) I felt the presence of the Holy Spirit in me. I gave my life to God here at YKCC. Please pray for my family and me."*

~G.B., INMATE AT YKCC

September 17, 2013—*"I'm writing to you because I watched your testimony in one of my treatment classes. I'm writing to you to ask for your prayers ."*

~B.K., INMATE AT YKCC

Conclusion

As a result of an impressive and growing harvest of good fruit, Abraham has become a well-known and sought-after evangelist in Alaska. He frequently receives invitations from all over Alaska and the Canadian – Yukon Territory. He is still traveling and telling of his celestial experiences and ministering by the power of the Holy Spirit. Hundreds of Alaskans have received salvation and physical, emotional and spiritual healing through Abraham George's powerful ministry.

SECTION TWO

MANY CONVINCING PROOFS

Introduction to
Section Two·

Was Abraham's claimed experience a genuine supernatural spiritual event? In this section, I have presented the array of proofs, which overcame my skepticism and brought me to a strong belief in its authenticity.

When confronted with spiritual or supernatural phenomena, we in the Western world are ill prepared to deal with it. This is due primarily to the fact that western thought has been dominated for decades by humanism—a materialistic and atheistic philosophy, which asserts (without evidence) that the material world is the only reality and that man is the highest authority in the universe. Carl Sagan, the renowned proponent of this dismal and audacious philosophy eloquently verbalized it stating: *"...the cosmos is all there is and all there ever will be."*

We have become so anesthetized by this deceptive philosophy that we are unaware of its distorting influence on our thinking. Therefore, if we encounter true spiritual or supernatural events, such as Abraham George's, the most common response is to give it negligible consideration or simply to reject it.

When I first heard Abraham's testimony, my mind was assaulted by an array of "western philosophy"-influenced, skeptical thoughts. I was tempted to just ignore what Abraham had said and to go on my "scientific-skeptical" way. However, I chose to keep an open mind and conduct my own investigation to uncover whatever evidence I might find. I'm glad I did, because I discovered many proofs supporting Abraham's claims.

In this section of the book, it will be argued that Abraham's claimed celestial experiences are **true** and can be **proven to be so.** "Proof" will be defined as the presentation of sufficient evidence so that an average and unbiased person would accept an assertion as proven or established as true. In court trials, it is referred to as "preponderance of evidence."

The basic argument being made is based on a fundamental law of physics known as the "law of causality," or as more commonly referred to, the "law of cause and effect." This law states that: "Every **effect** must have a **cause** that is equal to or greater than the observed effect." A simplified statement of this law is: "The **effect** is what happened and the **cause** is why it happened." The law of causality is universal in its application and is the basis for understanding nearly all interactions within the physical world.

The most logical "cause" sufficient to account for the amazing phenomena (effects) in Abraham's ministry is the one Abraham clearly presented within his testimony: *"I [Jesus] will be with you and my power will be with you."*

Author's Note: When I first heard Abraham make that statement—"I Abraham make that statement—"I will be with you and my power will be with you."—it was immediately obvious that I would only have to disprove that claim in order to discredit his entire testimony. Only a smattering of falsehood mingled with any amount of truth results in falsehood. However, to my amazement, I soon discovered that wherever Abraham had gone and presented his story, supernatural phenomena had accompanied him.

The wind and its effects on the natural world present an easily grasped illustration of this principle. When we gaze out our window and see trees swaying and leaves swirling down the street, what we are actually seeing are the **effects** of an invisible **cause** (the wind). This example of the wind also demonstrates that we commonly acknowledge the existence of realities which we cannot see—the apple fell to the ground **(effect)** because of gravity **(cause).** All the conclusions or "facts" of nuclear physics—atomic power plants, atomic bombs, etc.—rely upon the application of this law, even though no human has ever seen an atom.

This process of reasoning as a means to knowledge is one with which we are all familiar and to such an extent that we are mostly unaware of it. It is essential to grasp this principle as demonstrated by the wind in order to apprehend the power of the "proofs" presented in the forthcoming chapters.

Admittedly, we are here dealing with unrepeatable events and invisible realities—death (separation of spirit and body) and invisible spiritual and celestial realms. Therefore, in our argumentation, we will be presenting the tangible "effects" accompanying Abraham's post "out-of-body" experiences in order to establish or "see" the invisible, yet real underlying cause. In this section, we will be endeavoring to prove that Abraham's simple statement— *"My power will be with you"*—presents the most logical explanation of the supernatural occurrences accompanying his ministry.

This common principle of reasoning, illustrated by the wind will be alluded to frequently throughout the remainder of the book as: "THE WIND IS BLOWING." This phrase will appear following each presentation of a significant effect, which is beyond natural explanation. When encountering forces or events (effects) which are undeniably beyond natural causation, there must, of necessity be (law of causality) a "super-natural cause."

The first proof which will be presented is: "THE PROOF OF THE MEDICAL EVIDENCE."

Chapter 9

THE PROOF OF
THE MEDICAL EVIDENCE

THE TESTIMONIES OF MEDICAL FIRST RESPONDERS
IN MANOKOTAK

MELVIN ANDREW, VPSO

The first medically trained person in Manokotak to examine and evaluate Abraham George on the day of his accident was Melvin Andrew, VPSO (Village Public Safety Officer). As village VPSO, Melvin received special training to provide emergency medical treatment and to be able to evaluate the nature and severity of injuries or medical conditions to determine the level of treatment necessary. His account of Abraham's condition a few hours after his accident follows:

> *"I attempted to get Abraham George to respond to verbal commands and physical contact. He just groaned and did not respond to commands. There was a visiting doctor in the village—Dr. Richard O'Connell from Dillingham. Dr. O'Connell said he may have one or more rib bones broken and needed medevac. The local CHAs and the doctor kept timely vitals of Abraham George; each time their facial expressions and words grew dim. Abraham George was dying a slow death. Finally, the EMS plane arrived. We loaded Abraham George in the plane. By this time his vitals were erratic and clearly not far from death. I believed he would die from his injuries. As soon as the plane took off, I told the person next to me*

that 'He is not coming home alive, but in a casket.'"

~Melvin Andrew

SALLY NUKWAK, CHA *(COMMUNITY HEALTH AIDE)*
Sally Nukwak, CHA and long term resident of Manokotak, provided her assessment of Abraham's condition: *"I was one of the health aides who assisted when Abraham had his accident and I thought he wouldn't make it due to the severity of his injuries."*

Abraham Testifies of His Injuries

The first time I heard Abraham describe the extent and severity of his injuries incurred from his accident, I was truly skeptical of his claims. To me it sounded as if he had been hit by a Mack truck at 60-miles-an-hour. I reasoned that if what Abraham had reported was actually true, he should have died instantly or soon thereafter. I was amazed that he survived.

Alaska Native Medical Center Discharge Summary

At that moment Abraham held up a copy of his one-page official Medical Discharge form[1] and read the extensive list of his injuries: "multiple rib fractures, L3 to L4 vertebrae fractures, pelvic fracture, respiratory failure, liver laceration." He handed out copies, and I was quick to grab one and to begin reading it over carefully. Two facts immediately struck me—first, that it undeniably confirmed Abraham's statements. And the second was a shocking three-part statement: "ADMITTED: 11/30/2005; DISCHARGED: 12/27/2005; CONDITION ON DISCHARGE: 'GOOD'." That totaled only **28** days. At that moment I was certain that something miraculous had occurred. The question for me at that moment was not IF something beyond the natural had occurred—but WHAT had occurred? My interest took a quantum leap forward.

After I had procured all of Abraham's medical records, I ended up with an imposing, inch-and-one-half thick pile of pages, filled with technical medical jargon. I immediately realized that I would need assistance to

---

1   *I have provided an unedited copy of Abraham's Discharge form in the appendix, pg. 182.*

decipher its contents to be able to accurately comprehend and report the true extent and severity of Abraham's injuries. I enlisted the services of Annette Hutton, a medical coding specialist, with 30 years' experience. She graciously agreed to read through and interpret the imposing stack of papers and then to provide me a one-page condensed report in layman's language. Her report is presented below.

MEDICAL RECORDS INTERPRETATION IN LAYMAN'S TERMS

FRACTURE ILIUM- BROKEN PELVIC GIRDLE BONE
BRACHIAL PLEXUS INJURY- DAMAGED NERVE SPINE
FRACTURE SACCRUM/COCCYX-BROKEN TAILBONE
LIVER LACERATION-TEARING OF ORGAN WITHOUT CUTTING

PNEUMOHEMOTHORAX- *AIR AND BLOOD ESCAPED IN TO CHEST CAVITY*

FRACTURED RIBS X SEVEN- *BROKEN RIB CAGE BONES*

FRACTURE LUMBAR VERTEBRA- BROKEN BACK BONE
ACUTE RESPIRATORY FAILURE- FAILURE TO BREATHING FUNCTION
PNEUMONIA- INFECTION OF LUNGS
HEMATURIA- BLOOD IN URINE
SUBQUTANEOUS EMPHYSEMA-AIR TRAPPED UNDER SKIN
ALCOHOL ABUSE-DRUNK-CHRONIC CONDITION
PLEURAL EFFUSION- WATER AROUND LUNGS
POST HEMORRAGHIC ANEMIA- ANEMIA DUE TO BLOOD LOSS
LUNG CONTUSION- BRUISED LUNG TISSUE
FRACTURE SCAPULA- BROKEN COLLAR BONE
FOREIGN BODY BRONCHUS- ABNORMAL LUNG FINDINGS
CONTUSION ABDOIMINAL WALL- BRUISED BELLY
HIGH BLOOD PRESSURE- CHRONIC CONDITION
ASTHMA- CHRONIC LUNG CONDITION-
TOBACCO ABUSE-CIGARETTE SMOKER

Interpreted by Annette Hutton, Coding Specialist

From this report I learned that Abraham's injuries were even more extensive than what the Discharge statement had indicated.

On December 27, 2005, Abraham was released from the Alaska Native Medical Center—only 28 days after his admission, carrying his Discharge form declaring his physical condition: "Good." He walked out the door on his own two feet into a new life. One he had never known before and could not even have imagined!

Chapter 10

THE PROOF OF
THE THREE KEY WITNESSES

Eileen George   *Bishop "Doc" Nicholson*   *Melvin Andrew, VPSO*

F rom ancient times, the telling force of three witnesses has been an accepted standard for establishing the truth of a claim or an accusation. As early as 1500 BC, the world renowned ancient Hebrew lawgiver, Moses, wrote: *"On the testimony of two or three witnesses a person is to be put to death, but no one is to be put to death on the testimony of only one witness."* In the first century, another famous writer and scholar re-stated this timeless principle:

> *"Every matter must be established by the testimony of two or three witnesses"*

> ~APOSTLE PAUL[1]

There is significant apologetic value in having three witnesses as opposed to only one, especially if the witnesses' perspectives and viewpoints are unique. To clarify, imagine an accident occurring at an intersection.

---

1   *2 Corinthians 13:1 (NIV) "Every matter must be established by the testimony of two or three witnesses."*

If three people standing on three opposing corners of the intersection witness the accident and their testimonies concur, there is a far greater likelihood of absolute accuracy of knowing what really took place, than if there were only one witness to the accident.

The definition of "key witness" as being used in this chapter is someone who has credibility, has been an eyewitness to what they are testifying, and whose involvement with Abraham has been unique and strategic. Each of the three witnesses possess these qualifications. Each of these witnesses possess extraordinary credentials and have unique perspectives. Together they provide substantial and persuasive proof corroborating Abraham's claims.

THE FIRST KEY WITNESS:
EILEEN GEORGE, ABRAHAM'S WIFE

Eileen George

Eileen George is full-blooded Yup'ik Eskimo and is originally from the village of Manokotak. She is a short, stocky woman with tan skin and a rounded face which is typical for most Eskimos. Eileen wears a perpetual, contagious warm smile which conceals her strong will and assertive personality. Eileen is quite verbal and doesn't leave one guessing for long as to what her true feelings or opinions are. She has been married to Abraham George for over 25 years and is the mother of their four grown children. Eileen fully engages in and enjoys the native subsistence lifestyle and rises to the peak of personal happiness when cutting up game meat, curing salmon or picking wild berries. I've jokingly nicknamed her "the world's greatest berry-picker," which always arouses a chuckle. The Eileen George

Eileen George cutting up walrus.

of today is drastically unlike the person she was prior to Abraham's incident in 2005. As witnessed by Manokotak resident, Arlene Franklin: *"Eileen was an unhappy and angry woman who hated her husband, frequently cursing him privately and publicly... a hopeless alcoholic who would often abandon her children to go on week-long drinking binges."* Eileen's self-confession of her condition then was: *"Alcohol became my idol and I was out of control."*

THE ATTRIBUTES WHICH QUALIFY EILEEN GEORGE TO BE A KEY WITNESS

From the onset of my research I was confident that Abraham's wife was going to be a crucial witness in my pursuit of the truth about Abraham and his story. There were several reasons for me to believe this. First, because she would obviously know more about her long-term marriage partner than anyone else. Second, due to having lived with him both before and after his accident, she would be a qualified and trustworthy judge of his claims. Third, because of her privileged and intimate relational knowledge, she would also be the most difficult person in the world for Abraham to hoodwink. For these reasons I was looking forward with great anticipation to the day when I would have the opportunity to interview Eileen George.

ABRAHAM'S UNWELCOMED HOMECOMING

When the "new and healed Abraham" arrived home in January, 2006, Eileen was anything but elated to see him, nor was she at all interested in hearing about his unearthly experiences and personal transformation. Her reception was as cold as ice.

When Abraham poured out his heart to tell her all that he had experienced, her response was guarded and extremely skeptical. It soon escalated into anger and then complete rejection of both Abraham and his story. The more Abraham spoke about his celestial experiences, the more agitated Eileen became. Her entire way of life—free-spirited carousing, drunkenness, and living irresponsibly—was being threatened by her husband's presence, loving words and behavior.

A verbal "war" ensued and Eileen was on the offensive. Eileen's self-confession was: *"I was out of control, desiring this world's sins. I didn't want to let go of the earthly things. I was cursing and cussing at my husband because of his work."* She locked her heels and became Abraham's first and foremost skeptic and antagonist in the village. She was unrelenting in her verbal assault, inwardly attempting to "push Abraham over the edge," which had always been easy to do **before**. Regardless of how provocative her words and actions were, Abraham remained calm, peaceful, and non-retaliatory. He would only retreat and pray for her. Melvin Andrew observed this remarkable un-Abrahamic behavior saying: *"Abraham patiently prayed for his wife, who at the time was still worldly and still openly against him."* Melvin later testified that Abraham's mild and forgiving response strongly influenced his acceptance of Abraham's testimony, saying: *"Abraham is genuine and truthful in his testimony."*

Eileen's castigation was loud and relentless and before long the entire village became aware of it. Melvin Andrew was an "ear-witness" to her ranting and stated: *"Eileen also would get on the village VHF radio network and publicly castigate and embarrass Abraham, calling him a liar, a hypocrite and a devil, and openly spoke of his shameful past."*

In the midst of her fuming, Eileen was also surreptitiously scrutinizing Abraham's every action and word, searching for and even hoping to uncover a flaw, a contradiction, or anything to discredit him and his disturbing unearthly claims.

One day she overheard neighbors excitedly discussing "healing miracles" which were occurring around Manokotak due to her husband's prayers. This was even more alarming and intensified her fears and anger. She responded by obstinately continuing her verbal siege and stepping up the frequency of her binge-drinking trips to Dillingham. A neighbor shared her "over-the-fence" observations of Eileen's behavior at this time:

"She was still drinking a lot and wasn't slowing down after his accident. His wife was against what he did at first, and I thought she was more impossible than he was, to stop drinking"
~SALLY NUKWAK

EILEEN'S JOURNEY TO ACCEPTANCE
OF ABRAHAM'S TESTIMONY

It is important to be aware that Eileen did not come to an acceptance of Ipli's claims quickly or easily—it was a long, agonizing journey for both her and her husband. Eileen's journey to belief of Abraham's testimony occurred simultaneously with her own spiritual pilgrimage to a radical **lifestyle** change. The two progressed simultaneously and were mutually supportive. As her spiritual perspective and condition improved, she became increasingly more open and inclined to seriously consider and ponder the barrage of startling reports she was hearing about her husband.

It was obvious to her that Abraham had a new-found love and concern for her, their children, and others. Witnessing her husband's genuine transformation was incomprehensible, and yet undeniable. Eileen confessed: *"He was a new man!"* **Abraham's changed lifestyle was the most significant contributing factor in her journey to acceptance.**

Another substantial factor influencing Eileen's eventual acceptance were the many miraculous healings, which she had personally witnessed as a result of Abraham's prayers. Day after day she saw and heard Abraham praying for those who came to their door. It seemed like if he wasn't praying for a neighbor, he was clutching his cell phone to his ear, praying for someone near or far. *"Many still visit him at his home asking for prayer"* (Melvin Andrew). As time passed, Eileen, primarily out of curiosity, occasionally accompanied Abraham on ministry trips to other villages where she witnessed even more healings.

Then during the 2007 Spiritual Feast in Manokotak, Eileen had another unearthly and unnerving experience. While sitting in a pew and watching her husband praying for people at the front of the church, she was awes when Abraham's face suddenly began to glow with an uncanny luminescence! She rubbed her eyes to be sure she was seeing clearly – the glow remained. It gave her some assurance when she realized that many others around her were also seeing the strange phenomena. She reported: *"The children were running up to Ipli and asking him, 'How come your face is glowing?'"* Melvin Andrew said: *"I saw Ipli's face different than before. His face had an aura I cannot properly explain in my limited tongue."* When Abraham finally sat down beside Eileen, she said: *"He was still glowing! I moved over and just sat there staring at his face!"* She wondered about its cause and significance. This experience made an indelible impression on her and it was another significant factor bringing her closer to embracing her husband's claims.

Eileen gradually began to see a connection and continuity between Abraham's story and its fruit—they were both beyond any explanation she could come up with. It caused her to consider Abraham's oft-repeated explanatory statement— *"Jesus told me: 'I will be with you and my power will be with you.'"*—as a plausible cause of his radical changes as well as the bizarre and unexplainable occurrences which had been taking place.

A LIFE-CHANGING CALL FROM A COMPLETE STRANGER

In September 2007, Eileen received an unusual and unexpected phone call from a woman in Bethel, Alaska, whom she had never met. It was unlike any call she had ever received before. That call was both disturbing and convicting and was destined to dramatically alter her life. Eileen spoke of it saying: *"It was Saturday when I called up my husband, and anger took over me. I was cursing and cussing at my husband and hung up the phone on him. About an hour and a half later, a lady from Bethel called me saying, 'I have a message from God for you'. She told me she didn't know me, and didn't know my name, but had a message for me which God had spoken to her in a dream: **'Tell Eileen not to stir up the storm, and don't hide from God and the Holy Spirit.'"***

That call rocked Eileen to her core—inwardly she knew it was a genuine word from God. Eileen later commented about it saying: *"That message opened up my eyes and my heart, and was real and new in my life. I understood the message—I was doing evil things, being jealous, angry, being a drunkard, out of control, but most of all cursing and cussing at my husband because of his work."*

That call literally "scared the **hell** out of her." It turned out to be the final straw that broke the back of her persistent rebelliousness and open resistance to God and her husband. Soon after that call, Eileen surrendered her tormented and tumultuous soul to Jesus Christ. That decision was the coup de grace of her resistance to Abraham's ministry and the beginning of fully joining him, not only as a 100% believer, but also a supporter and traveling partner.

THE TELLING TESTIMONY OF ABRAHAM GEORGE'S WIFE

It wasn't until 2011 that I finally caught up with Eileen to interview her. The interview lasted only an hour, but it provided invaluable information, all supporting Abraham's authenticity. I had several prepared questions to ask her. Excerpts from that telling interview are included below.

INTERVIEW BEGINS: *"Eileen, tell me about Abraham George prior to his accident in 2005."* Immediately I noticed a dramatic change in her countenance—her perpetual smile gave way to somberness and sadness; then a few tears welled up in her eyes as she began lamenting her dark memories of her husband's long-term and painful abuse. She told about his recurring week-long drinking binges and his frequent verbal, mental, and physical beatings which often followed. I was shocked when she spontaneously added: *"As a matter of fact, when I heard about his accident, I was hoping he would die!"*

SECOND QUESTION: *"Eileen, when Abraham returned to Manokotak in January, 2006, did you believe his incredible story?"* Without hesitation she blurted out: *"NO!"* From what she had just revealed about the anguish she had suffered in their chronically dysfunctional marriage, I would have been surprised—even skeptical—if she had answered otherwise. I judged her response as both logical and true to life, for she had plenty of reasons to reject her husband's claims besides the universal natural human skepticism and aversion to anything supernatural.

THIRD QUESTION: *"Eileen, five years have now passed since Abraham came home claiming to have met Jesus and being taken by him on a tour of heaven and hell. Do you believe his story at this time?"* She instantly and boldly blurted out: *"YES, I do!"*

FOURTH QUESTION: *"What factors or events caused you to change your mind?"* She responded: *"He was really changed. He never ever hit me after that. He never called me names. He quit his drinking. He was a new man and he began traveling."*

FIFTH QUESTION: *"Eileen, if in the future Abraham should become an evangelist traveling the world, what would you do?"* Her answer was spontaneous and definite: *"I would go with him!"* That she was telling the truth was apparent because she had already been traveling with her husband on several mission trips to various Alaskan villages.

THE "NEW" EILEEN GEORGE

Following her surrender to God, Eileen felt peace and calm for the first time for as long as she could remember. She immediately began to experience tangible changes in her internal vision, attitude and behavior. After nearly 20 years of enslavement to alcohol, in October, 2007, Eileen took her last drink and has remained sober ever since. Profound changes soon became evident to all. Manokotak resident, Arlene Franklin, commented on Eileen's amazing transformation: *"Eileen doesn't drink alcohol anymore. She has improved in being a mother—taking care of her children and grandchildren. She loves to read the Bible. She tells about Jesus and the Bible anywhere to anyone. She's a lady who's on fire for Jesus!"* Eileen's grown daughter, Allison, commented: *"She doesn't drink alcohol anymore and goes to church."*

> "I THOUGHT ME AND MY HUSBAND HAD NO HOPE. WE WERE CHAINED UP. WE THOUGHT WE WOULD BE TRAPPED THE REST OF OUR LIVES."
>
> ✧❈✧
>
> Eileen

CONCLUSION

Eileen's reversal from complete rejection to full acceptance of Abraham's testimony came about in spite of her determined efforts to reject it and adamant refusal to believe it. Her change of mind came about incrementally, albeit grudgingly. It was the weight of the cumulative evidence and influence of numerous factors which she encountered on her two-year journey from denial to acceptance. This means that the experiential evidence Eileen encountered was so real and convincing that it overcame her stubborn unwillingness to believe. This fact adds substantial weight to her testimony.

Eileen now frequently travels with Abraham on his mission trips around Alaska. She boldly declares: *"The future for me is like in the Bible to 'Go spread the message.' I'm going to be with him!"* Melvin Andrew witnessed and acknowledged this profound turnaround, saying: *"Now she is sharing her testimony in church and traveling with her husband! Today she is a Spirit-filled help for Abraham."*

THE WIND IS BLOWING.

Eileen singing with Abraham in Kiana, Alaska

Abraham speaking in Kiana, Alaska.

SECOND KEY WITNESS:
BISHOP WILLIAM NICHOLSON

Bishop William "Doc" Nicholson was born and raised in Dillingham, in Southwestern Alaska. He is a genetic blend of Danish and Yup'ik Eskimo. He is a husky guy with a warm friendly smile. He is most commonly addressed as simply "Doc" by those who know him—a nickname he received as a youth from a neighbor after he had bandaged up his son from a knife-wound accident.

Doc tends to be more pragmatic than philosophical in his approach to ministry. He is not only a man of the heart, but also of the mind: *"If indeed there is a movement of the Holy Spirit and renewal going on in our midst, we must use our minds, not only our hearts."*

Bishop "Doc" Nicholson

Doc is known and respected in Southwestern Alaska as a dedicated leader in the Moravian denomination and also because he has been a Bristol Bay commercial fisherman for many years.

THE ATTRIBUTES WHICH QUALIFY BISHOP NICHOLSON AS A KEY WITNESS

By Alaska standards Doc is a highly educated man, having earned a bachelor's degree from George Fox College and a Master's of Divinity degree from the Moravian Theological Seminary in Bethlehem, Pennsylvania.

Bishop Nicholson is a man of impeccable character, credibility and reputation. He served as a part-time chaplain in the Alaska and Idaho Army National Guard for 11 years, receiving an honorable discharge in 2009. He also served on the Board of Trustees for the Alaska Moravian

96

Seminary from 1998 to 2008. Doc was appointed as a Presbyter of the Moravian Church in 2001 and ordained as "second" bishop of the Alaska Moravian Church in 2008.

BISHOP NICHOLSON'S JOURNEY TO ACCEPTANCE OF ABRAHAM'S TESTIMONY

Bishop Nicholson's initial involvement with Abraham George began in December 2005. When returning from active deployment to Iraq, one of his first civilian pastoral duties was to respond to Abraham's family request to pray for him at the native hospital in Anchorage. This was while Abraham was hospitalized from his fateful snowmobile accident. Then, less than a month later, Doc was shocked when he began hearing reports that Abraham not only had survived his physical ordeal, but he was now actually leading a spiritual revival in Manokotak. Doc reported: *"I heard—astonishingly—how this guy was now winning souls for the kingdom. I heard of many young people in Manokotak turning their lives over to Christ. Folks who would have never entertained going to church were now filling the Moravian Church. This struck me as very unusual."*

Doc was both intrigued and perplexed by the reports concerning Abraham. He maintained a guarded skepticism of them, however, until he could personally confirm them. At this time he was serving as an ordained Presbyter of the Moravian Church. He felt a solemn responsibility to be cautious about his appraisal of Abraham, for he realized that his credibility and reputation would certainly be affected by any decisions or statements he made.

He knew that as soon as possible he would have to make an accurate, informed and definitive decision about Abraham, stating: *"It was imperative that I finalized my judgment of Ipli by meeting with him face-to-face privately."* Doc, therefore, scheduled a personal interview with Abraham and barraged him with an array of defining questions. As a result of that interview, Doc's apprehensions and concerns were allayed and he stated: *"I finalized my judgment of Ipli by meeting with him privately face-to-face… I was convinced—or rather convicted—by the 'proof in the pudding.' What convinced me of his credibility as a spokesman for God was that he gave Christ the glory. I sensed a great brokenness and* *humility before the Lord—a real dependence upon the Lord. I left the interview feeling that **this man is the** real thing and God will continue to use him."*

Doc was so impressed and confident of Ipli's credibility and genuineness as a result of that interview, that he single-handedly organized the first-ever "Spiritual Feast" in Anchorage, featuring Abraham George as keynote speaker. He reported: *"In the winter of 2008, I arranged a three-night rental of the First Congregational Church in order to accommodate the large anticipated crowds. Sure enough, the sanctuary was loaded with people. The fruits of that first night after Ipli spoke, was a blessing; souls were won and recommitted to the Savior. It appeared to be a move of God. I was left feeling: 'How could I discredit this man?'"*

Based on the fruitful results of the Anchorage Spiritual Feast, combined with what Doc had previously determined from his personal interview with Abraham, Doc came to a determination and personal conviction about Abraham and his testimony, declaring: *"I affirm that Abraham George is a man of humility and personal integrity. I believe, along with many others, that Abraham George has had a legitimate, though incredible, 'out-of-body' experience in which he was given a personal message by Jesus Christ himself to share wherever he would be invited. Abraham's life has truly been transformed, which has been attested to by many witnesses. I believe that Abraham's experience is genuine and that God will continue to use him mightily." (March 11, 2008).* THE WIND IS BLOWING.

THE EXCOMMUNICATION OF BISHOP WILLIAM NICHOLSON

I first met Bishop "Doc" Nicholson during the Spiritual Feast in Manokotak in October 2008 on my first investigative trip there. I was pleasantly surprised to find that although I had been told that he was a "Bishop of the Church," he was neither pompous nor religiously starchy as I had suspected. On the contrary, Doc blended in with the rest of the participants and wholeheartedly and jubilantly entered into all the spontaneous spiritual festivities (some of which, I suspected, surely must have "stretched" his traditional theology). I felt an instant rapport and respect for him. He seemed to prefer to be addressed simply as "Doc."

Little could he or anyone have imagined that his participation in that Spiritual Feast and his blessing and encouragement of it would soon bring him to a "Y-in-the-road" decision encompassing his theology, his position, and his life-calling.

Author's Note: Bishop Nicholson was ordained in 2008, as one of four Bishops of the Alaska Moravian Church. He served in that capacity until 2011 when he was summarily removed from that office, due to his support of Abraham George and the Spiritual Feast movement. His statements quoted in this book were made while he still officially held the office of Bishop, unless stated otherwise.

When Doc arrived back in Anchorage from that landmark Manokotak gathering, he was overflowing with joy and excitement and felt compelled to share his perceptions and experiences with the other key Moravian leaders. He sent them a heartfelt message saying: *"The Manokotak Spiritual Feast was an eye-opener for me as to what God may be doing for revival in the hearts of Moravians in rural Alaska. For days after attending the Manokotak Feast, my heart was full of rejoicing and appreciation for what God has done. To this day, over three weeks later, my heart still remains touched. Indeed something beyond the norm, something very different and very real may be happening to our beloved church. I came to this realization after attending what everyone is now calling a 'Spiritual Feast.'"* That message would prove to be a "destiny bombshell" not only for his own life, but for the entire Moravian denomination in Alaska.

Bishop Nicholson's experience in Manokotak brought about an immediate paradigm shift in his ministry focus. He began spending substantial time supporting, promoting, and defending the ministry of Abraham George and the growing Spiritual Feast movement.

Doc was dismayed and painfully disheartened when he soon received a message from his peers—the presbyters and the first bishop of the Alaska Moravian Church—strongly suggesting that he abandon his involvement with Abraham George and unite with them in renouncing him as "a false prophet and antichrist." They also insisted that he immediately discontinue his involvement and promotion of the Spiritual Feast movement, due to *"...actions contrary to the beliefs and doctrinal practices of the Alaska*

Moravian Church" (Alaska Provincial Board President, Rev. Peter Green).

Doc initially simply ignored their suggestions as mere temporary expressions of ruffled religious feathers. Unfortunately, the hierarchal "suggestions" only increased in frequency and force. Doc then began in earnest a serious apologetic dialogue, defending biblically the legitimacy of Abraham and the Spiritual Feast movement. His words, however, fell on deaf ears. After months of written and emailed theological dialogue between the other Moravian leaders and himself, nothing changed.

Then in 2009, an official Moravian Synod was convened. The focus of the Synod was primarily on the growing and divisive issue of the new Spiritual Feast movement and Abraham George. It especially addressed the support and involvement of Bishop Nicholson with them. The Synod ultimately mandated the "cessation of Spiritual Feasts in all Moravian churches in Alaska." Doc, however, remained resolute because he perceived that the issue was more than a mere disagreement over religious dogma and practices contrary to the historical and traditional church. In his mind and heart he saw a profoundly significant matter of truth regarding what he strongly believed was a genuine visitation of God through the Holy Spirit. Therefore to Doc, it was non-negotiable. The hierarchal messages escalated to threats of reprisal, unless he "cease and desist from agreeing with, promoting, or being involved with the Spiritual Feast movement."

Finally, Bishop Nicholson received an official written final reprimand titled: "Letter regarding Synod and directive." It read as follows:

> *"Rev. William Nicholson: The 2009 Provincial Synod mandated that the concept of 'Spiritual Feasts' discontinue within the Moravian churches; again in synod 2010, it was reconfirmed that there be no such gathering within Moravian congregations. You have been repeatedly told to discontinue encouraging and supporting actions contrary to the beliefs and doctrinal practices of the Alaska Moravian Church. Therefore, after prayerful deliberation the APB concluded with the following action: to terminate you from your pastoral duties in the Anchorage Moravian church and any other*

relating duties within the Alaska Moravian church effective at the end of your current ministerial contract. Members of the Alaska Provincial Board of the Alaska Moravian Church.”

~DOCUMENT SIGNED BY THE REV. PETER GREEN,
*PRESIDENT OF THE ALASKA PROVINCIAL BOARD
OF THE MORAVIAN CHURCH*

Bishop William Nicholson was thus officially defrocked; his life long career with the Alaska Moravian church was ended; his income was cut off; the denomination he grew up in, was educated in, faithfully served in, and dearly loved—had now expelled him. When asked about his sentiment regarding this tragic and painful consequence, Doc calmly affirmed: *"I was willing to fear God more than man."* THE WIND IS BLOWING.

THE FRACTURING OF A DENOMINATION

The controversy over Abraham and the Spiritual Feast movement unfortunately didn't end with the removal of Bishop Nicholson from office, as the Moravian church leadership had hoped. After his removal, Doc, along with numerous other like-minded believers, persisted in supporting Abraham and the Spiritual Feast. This eventually resulted in the excommunication of Bishop William Nicholson and his entire Anchorage congregation, as well as Abraham George and the Manokotak congregation.

Several months after that edict, Doc Nicholson, along with a large entourage of other believers, made a direct appeal to the International Moravian Unity Board in

Author's Note: Why would anyone in their right mind— especially such an educated, reputable and influential man as Bishop William Nicholson—cleave to a controversial position that knowingly could possibly result in such catastrophic personal consequences? Doc seemingly had nothing to gain and everything to lose for taking the hard stand which he did.

The true answer that Doc Nicholson set forth was spoken, written and finally, vividly displayed to the world, when he accepted its painful consequence— he BELIEVED! What level of certainty regarding Abraham's legitimacy do Doc's actions indicate? The apologetic value of Doc's testimony is incalculable! A gale force wind has blown!

Herrnhut, Germany. A small Alaskan delegation was appointed to travel to Germany and present their case in person, verbally and in writing to the international leaders. The end result of their appeal was that the International leaders acknowledged the legitimacy of their claims and in November 2012 granted their request to form a new Alaskan Moravian denomination, called "United Alaska Moravian Ministry," with Bishop William Nicholson serving as its President. **Truth does not bend or bow when assaulted; it only becomes more evident.** THE WIND IS BLOWING.

THE THIRD KEY WITNESS: MELVIN ANDREW

Melvin Andrew was born in Akiachak, Alaska, during the summer fish

Melvin Andrew, State Trooper of the Year Award 2001, Manokotak VPSO for 20 years

camp in 1963. He is the son of a well-known and respected Moravian pastor, John Andrew Sr. Melvin is full-blooded Yup'ik Eskimo and grew up in a variety of Alaska native villages including: Akiachak, Tuluksak, Manokotak, Kongiganak, and Bethel. Manokotak has been his home since 1985, where he and his wife Sally have raised their eight children. After completing high school, Melvin applied for the Alaska State Troopers VPSO (Village Public Safety Officer) Training Program.[2] After receiving approval from the Manokotak Village Council, the regional Native Corporation, and the State Troopers, he enrolled in the intensive training program and graduated in 1985.

2 According to the troopers, in this training, "A VPSO learns about law enforcement, first aid, firefighting and other public safety issues by attending a ten-week VPSO Academy... Village Public Safety Officers (VPSOs) are dedicated, concerned citizens living in rural areas within Alaska who assist their villages in all aspects of public safety. VPSOs do not carry firearms, although they are trained with non-lethal weapons, such as pepper spray and expandable batons. VPSOs are generally the first to respond to calls for help from community members, hence their motto: 'First Responders—Last Frontier'" (Alaska State Troopers website: http://www.dps.state.ak.us/ast/vpso).

QUALIFICATIONS OF MELVIN ANDREW AS A KEY WITNESS

Melvin Andrew possesses an array of qualifications which make him an extremely valuable and credible witness regarding Abraham George's testimony.

Melvin moved to Manokotak in 1985, and the same year began serving as VPSO. He then served as village VPSO in Manokotak for the next 20 years. VPSOs serve a critical role in contemporary Alaskan native village life, where they essentially serve the role of both sheriff and medical doctor. They are the only resident law enforcement in nearly all the outlying villages scattered across Alaska's vast 586,000 square miles. They work with the State Troopers, enforcing state laws and local ordinances.

Melvin is one of the most well-known and respected men in Manokotak. He has been a community leader since his arrival in 1985 as VPSO. In 2001, Melvin received the distinguished State of Alaska "VPSO of the Year Award." His integrity and moral character have been confirmed by the spiritual leaders of Manokotak, who over the years have appointed Melvin to a variety of responsible positions in the local church, including: youth leader, Sunday school director and Elder. In 1998 Melvin enlisted in the Alaska Army National Guard and graduated with honors from Officer Candidate School and served in the Guard until 2001. Mr. Andrew was most recently honored by being elected as Mayor of Manokotak.

Because of Melvin's 20-year career as VPSO, which overlapped Abraham George's residency in Manokotak, he had many firsthand encounters with Abraham George both before and after his fateful accident in 2005. Melvin has provided a unique and invaluable perspective on many of the events in Abraham's story. As a law enforcement officer, he has verified Abraham's pre-2005 lawless, despicable character and behavior. As the most highly trained medical person in the village, he has provided vital facts about the severity of Abraham's injuries from his accident. He has corroborated the life transformations of both Abraham and his wife, Eileen. He has verified the genuineness of many miracles of healing in Manokotak and other places. He has been invaluable in quantifying the impact of Abraham's testimony and changed life on the village of

Manokotak. He has confirmed the nature and impact of the Spiritual Feast movement in Alaska.

MELVIN'S PRE-2005 INVOLVEMENT WITH ABRAHAM GEORGE

Melvin Andrew's involvement with Abraham George began shortly after becoming Manokotak's VPSO in 1985. Because he represented the law in that small village and Abraham was completely lawless, they were destined to have many clashes, which they did. Melvin knew Abraham at his worst and referred to him as a "drunk and lawbreaker." Over the years there were many dramatic, hands-on, face-to-face confrontations and frequent arrests. Melvin described one of them as follows: *"The worst experience with Abraham was when I went to arrest him on a warrant. Abraham was intoxicated at the time of arrest and resisted. Abraham was belligerent and combative. I had two tribal police officers assist me to physically restrain him to place handcuffs on him. In the process I had to utilize pepper spray to restrain and subdue him. We then had to carry him out of the house, place him in the patrol car and carry him to the local detention facility to await airplane transport to Dillingham."*

The relationship between Melvin Andrew and Abraham George deteriorated over the years to one of mutual disrespect, animosity and hatred. Whenever Abraham and Melvin met on the streets of Manokotak, Abraham would lambaste Melvin with verbal curses and crude vulgarities. Abraham issued a standing threat to Melvin that *"if he ever met him in the woods he would shoot him."* They were the worst of enemies.

On November 29, 2005, at 7:30 PM, twenty years after his first encounter with Abraham George, Melvin heard the following emergency announcement on the village VHF radio: "Person injured, VPSO and health aides needed immediately at the clinic!" He soon learned that the injured person was his nemesis, Abraham George, who had suffered a severe snow machine accident and had just arrived at the Manokotak clinic on a cargo sled. Melvin immediately notified the health aides and rushed to the clinic. Melvin was the first medical responder to examine Abraham at the clinic. As VPSO, he had received EMT (emergency medical training) to enable him to perform emergency aid and to evaluate traumatic injuries in order to determine what course of action or level of medical help would be required. Based on his assessment of Abraham's injuries, Melvin determined that Abraham's condition was most likely fatal: *"I believed he would die from his injuries."*

Melvin immediately called for a medevac plane from Dillingham. After the plane landed, Melvin stated: *"We loaded Abraham George into the plane. By this time his vitals were erratic and he was clearly not far from death. As soon as the plane took off, I told the person next to me that 'He is not coming back alive, but in a casket.' Deep inside I was happy he was not coming back—one less 'bad boy' to watch and deal with."* Melvin was inwardly celebrating as he watched the medevac plane take off from Manokotak. Finally, his long-time nemesis would be out of his life permanently—or so he hoped.

MELVIN'S JOURNEY TO ACCEPTANCE
OF ABRAHAM'S TESTIMONY

Melvin heard nothing more about Abraham until December 23, 2005. On that day, he reported hearing an announcement on the VHF radio by Eileen's family that: *"They were going to have life-support removed from Abraham and they requested prayers on his behalf."* Melvin stated: *"I still remember that day—it was December 23, 2005. I knew he was going to die!"*

Melvin figured that no doubt someday soon he would be hearing Abraham's funeral being announced on the radio. Then, three days later, to his shocked surprise, Melvin heard: ***"ABRAHAM IS ALIVE AND WALKING!"*** He was disturbed and perplexed, stating: *"I said in my mind, **'NO WAY! He's supposed to be dead!'** I was surprised to hear that Abraham George was awake and able to walk."*

The next news Melvin heard about Abraham really jolted him— *"I heard stories here and there that he went to hell and heaven while in a near-death situation. I didn't believe it one bit. Not him. I won't believe a drunk and law-breaker. I just called him one lucky SOB!"*

Then, in early January of 2006, Melvin received another stomach-twisting report about Abraham—his dreaded enemy had just disembarked from a plane at the Manokotak airport. Melvin couldn't believe it. He didn't **want** to believe it. He was certain that something really weird must have taken place.

> *"Abraham George came home in January, walking unassisted, limping, using crutches."*
>
> ~MELVIN ANDREW

Melvin was still reeling from the news of Abraham's extraordinary survival and quick healing. Now he had to deal with this awful news—Abraham was back walking the streets of Manokotak and under his jurisdiction.

Shortly after Abraham returned home, Melvin heard that Abraham was planning to tell about his whole ordeal on Saturday night at the church. He made a note to be sure he didn't miss it. By now he was filled with curiosity and had a multitude of questions about Abraham.

Melvin arrived at the church early and sat in the back row. His mind was assaulted with past memories and skepticism—he was on his guard. When Abraham began speaking, Melvin was taken aback by the air of authority in Abraham's voice—*"Abraham George prayed with boldness and authority I never knew."* He listened intently to his every word. Reflecting back on that night Melvin stated: *"I heard Abraham George's personal testimony for the first time that Saturday evening. Now I knew why he changed! Still, I was skeptical."* Due to the years of painful and violent encounters, Melvin was extremely doubtful of Abraham's unbelievable claims and was resolved that it would require a mountain of proof before he would ever believe that what he had just heard was true. From that night on, Melvin began scrutinizing Abraham's words and behavior, feeling certain that he would easily be able to find evidence that would disprove Abraham's claims. After several months, however, he surprisingly came up empty-handed. What Melvin did discover in his pursuit not only altered his belief about Abraham, but it also dramatically impacted his own life.

TESTIMONY OF ABRAHAM'S TRANSFORMATION
There were many factors and facts involved in Melvin Andrew's decision

to ultimately believe Abraham's testimony. It was a gradual process of months of inquiry, careful observation, lots of pondering, and *"many sleepless nights."* He was surprised by the fact that all the evidence seemed to support Abraham's crazy claims. The hard evidence eventually overcame his painful memories and skepticism. A sampling of that evidence follows.

The most convincing evidence of all for Melvin was Abraham's undeniably transformed life. Melvin acknowledged: *"The first change I noticed in Abraham was his physical countenance. Something unexplainable using any human words, but I'll try my best. He changed from his usual mischievous 'I'm-gonna-do-something-bad' smirk to a beautiful genuine 'I love you' and happy smile. The second was his constant acknowledgment of Jesus Christ and Him alone, in prayer or speech. There was no more 'Me' or 'Ipli-guyuk' [Yupik expression of self-pride], his usual prideful and self-righteous flaunting of his ability."*

Another factor which deeply affected Melvin was observing Abraham praying quietly and privately for his wife who had been publically ranting against him. He said he also noticed that Ipli began demonstrating a genuine concern and respect for his wife's personhood, which he had never done before.

Abraham's election into the office of Elder in the church and his faithful service in that capacity for three years also weighed in on his decision. Melvin's travels with Abraham were a huge eye-opening experience. He recalled: *"I traveled with him on three occasions to many villages: Togiak—2006, Kipnuk—2007, then Chevak, Hooper Bay, Scammon Bay, Bethel, Nunapitchuk, Kasigluk, Akiachak, Kwethluk and Akiak—being an eyewitness to him leading many to Christ Jesus... observing his humbleness to all, the rich, the poor, the saved and the sinner, the sick and those in bondage—he's a changed man! Clearly this man was true to what he was saying... Abraham is genuine and truthful in his testimony."*

The most convincing and powerful evidence of all for Melvin was Abraham's undeniably transformed life. Melvin stated: *"The most impressive was Abraham's changed life!"* and *"The most profound change* *is **lifestyle**, period!"*

Melvin summed up the reason for his conviction regarding Abraham's authenticity saying: *"I have to believe what I saw... I am totally convinced that Abraham has had a true visit from our Lord Jesus Christ and was given the task to tell His children a message... Abraham is genuine and truthful in his testimony. He is now a messenger to us with a specific message from the Lord Jesus Christ himself. **My life has changed because of what Jesus Christ did for Abraham.**"*

AN UNIMAGINABLE RELATIONSHIP IS BIRTHED

In the course of Melvin Andrew's ensuing months-long scrutiny of Abraham's lifestyle, he not only became a believer, but something unimaginable occurred—Melvin and Abraham became best friends. Melvin described this amazing new relationship saying: *"Abraham is now my **best friend** and co-worker in harvesting souls for Jesus! We laugh together; we cry together; we pray together no matter where we may be. One time he recognized me at Anchorage Wal-Mart and in the midst of shoppers, I heard our usual greeting, 'PRAISE THE LORD!' I looked around, located him with arms raised and yelled back, 'HALLELUJAH!'"*

Melvin and Abraham – now best friends!

Chapter 11
The Proof of a Radically Transformed Life

"You can fool some of the people all the time, all the people some of the time, but you can't fool all the people all the time."

~Abraham Lincoln

The proof of this chapter is based upon a fundamental law of physics known as Newton's "First Law of Motion," or, as it is most often referred to, "The Law of Inertia." This law states: *"A body in motion continues in motion with the same speed and in the same direction unless acted upon by a sufficient opposing force."*

It is self-evident that this principle also applies to human behavior for anyone who has ever struggled to overcome the momentum of an entrenched habit or a chronic addiction. Mustering up the "sufficient opposing force"—desire, will-power, determination, effort and stamina— to reverse the momentum of even one chronic habit or addiction can be a supremely and painfully difficult task.

Keeping the Newtonian principle in mind, imagine the magnitude of power sufficient to account for Abraham George's abrupt, dramatic and multifaceted lifestyle changes all occurring simultaneously. Abraham's verified changes included: the abandonment of long-term (20+years) drug and alcohol addictions, correcting major moral and ethical deficits, vocabulary transformation, adopting new husbanding and fathering skills, and major attitudinal and behavioral adjustments toward the law. It is the objective of this chapter to prove, by presenting multiple eyewitness testimony, that Abraham has, in fact, undergone a radical life transformation which lends powerful credence to his testimony.

How Bad Abraham Was Before 2005

Before November 29th, 2005, Abraham George was clearly a self-centered, angry, mean, hot-tempered, chronic drunkard and drug addict. He was feared and despised by his wife and nearly everyone else who knew him in his home village of Manokotak. Establishing the nefariousness of Abraham prior to 2005 was not a difficult task. Everyone that I've talked to over the past few years who knew him before 2005, have profusely described his badness in a variety of ways. The sentiments expressed below are an accurate portrayal of him:

"I wanted him to die because of the hatred I had for his abuse."
~EILEEN GEORGE
ABRAHAM'S WIFE

"Before the accident he was gone quite a lot, either in jail or drinking."
~ARLENE FRANKLIN
MANOKOTAK

"I've known Abraham 10+years. He was the downtown [Dillingham] drunk. He was arrested for criminal activity and drinking numerous times."
~SIRENA TENNYSON
DILLINGHAM, ALASKA

"Ever since I met him, before his accident, he and his wife would take turns having drinking binges for a week to nearly a month away from their kids. I would either see him or his wife drunk in Dillingham."
~SALLY NUKWAK
MANOKOTAK

"He used to fight with his wife. They were drunks."
~MOSES AYOJIAK
TOGIAK, ALASKA

"They'd be out of town for days at a time [on drinking binges] and it got to a point where he would be gone and then his wife would go... He had many encounters with the VPSOs [the law]."

~KEN NUKWAK
MANOKOTAK

"Abraham George was a 'crook' and a law-breaker, a drunk, pot smoker, wife-beater and womanizer. He caused pain and hardship to family and friends in the community and was an all-around nemesis to me, because I was law enforcement."

~MELVIN ANDREW
VPSO, MANOKOTAK

Prior to 2005, Abraham had already amassed a staggering court record with numerous entries.[1] In that record Abraham George is characterized as "a menace to society".

ABRAHAM'S RADICAL LIFE TRANSFORMATION

Abraham has remained out of jail and drug and alcohol free since 2005. He has become a renowned Christian spiritual leader, speaker and traveling evangelist to the native villages of Alaska.

ELECTION TO SPIRITUAL LEADERSHIP & VILLAGE COUNCIL

One of the weightiest authentications of Abraham's life transformation is the fact that in 2006 he was elected to the office of "Elder" in Manokotak's only church. In the cultural context of contemporary village life, this action was one of the highest possible public recognitions of Abraham's moral character and integrity. This election also clearly revealed an acknowledgment of his testimony claims. Surely they would not have appointed Abraham if they ever suspected him of being a public fraud. Abraham faithfully served the church in the office of Elder from 2006 to 2008.

In 2008 Abraham was also elected by community Council leaders to

---

1   See Appendix for copy of court record.

serve on the Village Council. This was another clear recognition of Abraham's dramatic lifestyle turnaround and a implicit agreement with his testimony. It further declares the Council leaders' esteem of Abraham's character and ability to make wise leadership decisions.

These two appointments to public office are of inestimable apologetic value in establishing Abraham's radical lifestyle change and in declaring the convictions of the community leaders regarding the validity of his claimed celestial experiences. These leaders were obviously aware of his reprehensible past, his accident and astonishing recovery, and had ample time and opportunity to observe his attitude and lifestyle since his return to the village in January 2006. The value and weight of this evidence could never be equaled by investigation or interviews.

EYEWITNESS TESTIMONIES CONFIRMING ABRAHAM'S RADICAL LIFE TRANSFORMATION

"Abraham George truly has undergone a dramatic life-transformation. This story may be a tale to some, but because of the unusual circumstances surrounding this man's life, he has been radically transformed with many firsthand witnesses... But more than those facts was the transformation of this former drunk and troublemaker. The greatest miracle, I felt, was Ipli standing up before the people and telling his story! Inside my spirit I felt confirmation."

~BISHOP WILLIAM NICHOLSON
ANCHORAGE

"Big changes in his life since the accident—like night to day."

~SIRENA TENNYSON
DILLINGHAM

"...when Abraham came home after the accident and his hospitalization he started talking about encounters with heaven and hell... Definitely his behavior and his speech changed... He went to church regularly when he got back. He showed me that people can sober up."

~KEN NUKWAK
MANOKOTAK

"People were skeptical that he changed, thinking he'd go back to drinking again, but no! He started traveling to villages soon after and a lot of villages were hungry to hear his testimony."

~SALLY NUKWAK
MANOKOTAK

"He has changed very much since the accident. He is with his family now."

~ARLENE FRANKLIN
MANOKOTAK

"We were in high school together in Akiachak. Last year I talked with Abraham. He is a really good guy now—a big change. When Abraham told his story [in Akiachak, his birth village], I believed him and the people there believed him — because he's changed."

~ESTHER SHEDLOSKY
ANCHORAGE

"The most impressive is Abraham's changed life... The most profound change is lifestyle, period. He's a changed man!"

~MELVIN ANDREW
VPSO, MANOKOTAK

CONCLUSION

It has been clearly demonstrated by the above eyewitness testimonies that Abraham George has indeed undergone a radical lifestyle transformation. This fact presents a crucial question which begs answering. In keeping with Newton's law of inertia, we are left to wonder what kind of "opposing force" could possibly account for such a drastic change of a lifetime of negative lifestyle momentum? It is my contention that a natural force or power capable of accounting for all of Abraham's lifestyle reversals does not exist. Logically this leaves only one other possibility—a supernatural or miraculous power, which is exactly what Abraham's testimony affirms.

If the facts presented in this chapter regarding Abraham's transformation were instead describing *your* own father, or *your* best friend, you would most assuredly be calling it a "miracle." You would be right, because there really is no other rational explanation. Abraham's oft-repeated explanation given in his testimony is sufficient to account for all the facts. It is the simplest, most reasonable also—*"Jesus told me, I will be with you and my power will be with you."* I strongly maintain that this is the true explanation of his radical changes and the many miracles present in his ministry.

THE WIND IS BLOWING.

Abraham & Eileen George's 25th Anniversary celebration, an event that NEVER would have happened.

Chapter 12
THE PROOF OF THE TESTIMONY OF MANOKOTAK

When I made the decision in February of 2008, to investigate Abraham George's testimony, I knew that a personal on-site visit to his home village of Manokotak would be required. Manokotak has been Abraham's home for the past 25 years; it is where the fateful snow machine accident occurred, and it's where Abraham has lived since his accident in 2005. It was obvious that Manokotak would be the logical place to begin my search for information from those who have been observing his life close-up before and after his experience and life transformation. I was confident that this village held important clues for or against Abraham's story and I was determined to find them.

Manokotak is a remote Yup'ik Eskimo village, situated in southwestern Alaska, and is accessible only by air or water. Manokotak is nestled between two low-lying, round-topped hills—like two camel humps—and the serene Igushik River.

This meandering and slow-moving river provides the village with water access to the ocean—a three-hour skiff ride down river to its mouth on the shores of pristine Bristol Bay.

Bristol Bay is world-renowned for its salmon-rich waters. Commercial salmon fishing has been Abraham's lifetime occupation and primary income to provide for his wife and four children and is the mainstay for

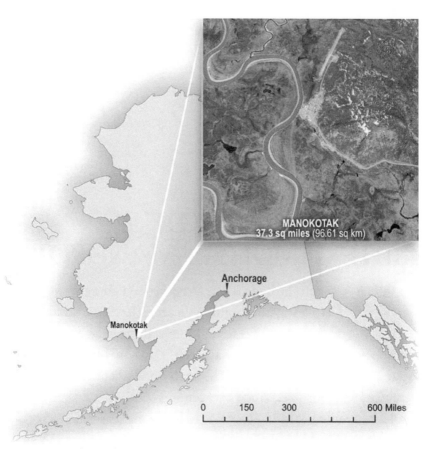

*Location of Manokotak, Alaska. INSET: Satellite view on the Igushik River
showing the airstrip from which Abraham was medevacked to Anchorage.*
Inset image ©2015 Digital Globe/Google Earth (date taken 5/24/2006)

Bristol Bay, renowned for vast salmon-rich commercial fishing
Image ©2015 Google Earth (date taken 4/9/2013)

Abraham George, commercial fisherman

nearly all of Manokotak's 450 residents.

Subsistence is a way of life in Manokotak. "Subsistence" is a household word among Alaskans and refers to the practice of "living off the land" by hunting, fishing, trapping, and gathering berries, firewood and other natural provisions. Subsistence has been the traditional native Alaskan way of life for generations and remains the norm for nearly all Alaskan villages today.

Manokotak has only one store which is operated by the local Native Corporation. It carries an extremely limited selection of clothing and groceries. Because everything must be flown in by small plane, prices are astronomically high. I have provided a sampling of recent grocery prices for your shocking enjoyment: *1-pound loaf white bread—$5.00; milk—$20.00/gallon; eggs—$5.00/dozen; pork chops— $10.75/pound.*

Manuquutaq (Manokotak) Trading Co.

Moravian missionaries were the first to arrive in Manokotak, so it thus became a Moravian village. The denominational orientation of the first missionary to arrive in a village generally determined its religious heritage. There are a wide spectrum of denominations represented in the native villages of Alaska. Manokotak has only one centrally located church building. The building has an auditorium equipped with wooden pews, three small classrooms, and no bathroom.

Manokotak has only a few short stretches of gravel roads and, like most other remote native villages, they are frequented by a scarcity of cars and trucks. Manokotak relies primarily on ATV's (all-terrain vehicles) and snow machines ("sno-gos") for day-to-day travel. On a typical day the roads of Manokotak are buzzing with an intermittent procession of four-wheelers or snow machines (depending on the season of year) coursing around the village. Everyone appears to be going somewhere.

Village of Manokotak on the Igushik River

Main Street, Manokotak

Manokotak homes

Manokotak residents riding 4-wheelers; a key component of village life

Abraham with walrus head and tusks. Every part is used for food and shared with villagers.

Manokotak's streets are sparsely lined with grey weathered or brightly painted, plywood-sided houses. Lots are spacious and strewn with a mixed array of boats and abandoned vehicles of every sort and vintage.

A treasury of "spare parts" – a valuable resource in village Alaska

Most residences also have equipment graveyards having a variety of worn-out, defunct, or partially dismantled ATVs, snow machines, and outboard motors. Because there is no parts store in Manokotak, these discarded machines are a treasury of readily available vital parts which are frequently scavenged and utilized to repair other machines.

Manokotak's chief nemesis, as with nearly all Alaskan native villages, is alcohol abuse. In spite of the fact that Manokotak is a "dry" village,[1] alcohol is readily available from the neighboring "wet" town of Dillingham where liquor sales are legal and booming. Due to the proximity of Dillingham—a mere 20 miles away—it is a convenient source of supply for Manokotak's unquenchable thirst for alcohol.

Every home in the village is equipped with a VHF radio that is turned on at every waking hour. This local radio network serves as a community bulletin board, announcing school lunch menus, sporting events, commuter plane arrivals, the arrival of the State Troopers, and of course,

---

1 *"Dry"—the production or sale of alcohol or alcoholic beverages is illegal.*

120

the latest juicy gossip. When Abraham experienced his accident, it was first announced to the community over this network. There are few secrets in Manokotak.

"VHF radios are on all the time, so we can't miss much."
~KEN NUKWAK,
LIFETIME RESIDENT OF MANOKOTAK

A high percentage of Manokotak's youth and adults seem to be on a par with average Americans when it comes to the use of and obsessions to TV, internet, videogames and electronic gizmos. Manokotak, as all Alaskan native villages, has been equipped with government-subsidized satellite television and Wi-Fi.

THE PROOF OF THE PHYSICAL EVIDENCE

My initial visit to Manokotak occurred in October, 2008. I chose that time because it allowed me to accomplish two important tasks at the same time. The first was to initiate my investigative book research at the place where it all began and it also allowed me to participate in the second annual "Spiritual Feast"[2] gathering which was scheduled for that three-day weekend.

I came to Manokotak with several specific goals in mind. First, I hoped to locate and photograph the remains of Abraham's snow machine and sled involved in his accident. Second, I wanted to get a first-hand geographic orientation of the locations and buildings mentioned in Abraham's testimony. Third, I wanted to meet and interview the residents of the community. I was particularly interested in locating and interviewing the people specifically mentioned in his story.

I discovered Abraham's fateful snow machine and sled in his private "used parts" area directly behind his house. The dilapidated old green Polaris snow machine which carried Abraham to his fateful accident was missing its right front ski and its hitch had obviously been wrenched off the rear bumper. The homemade sled was about 14 feet long and 4 feet wide and was made out of heavy wooden planks. It was equipped with

---

2   *See Chapter 8 for details about the "Spiritual Feast" movement.*

Y-harness on a sled

a strong, pivoting, Y-shaped towing yoke made from 1-inch steel pipe. The sled[3] was definitely sturdy enough to have hauled the "1500 pound load of firewood" specified by Abraham in his testimony.

The sno-go and sled were partially covered over by tall grass and brush and in the company of the remains of other junked snow machines, partially dismantled ATVs, and a variety of defunct outboard motors—some missing cowlings, others missing lower units. As I stood gazing upon the variety of abandoned equipment, I had the sentimental thought of how each of them were in a sense memorials of Abraham's family history—of past walrus, seal, caribou and moose hunts, and countless salmon catches during many summer fish camps.

Abraham's "sno-go" — missing right front ski

---

3   *See photo of sled in Chapter 1.*

I was satisfied that the surviving physical evidence definitely corroborated Abraham's descriptions of them in his testimony.

Abraham showing wrenched hitch on back of fateful "sno-go"

Rear view of "sno-go", showing wrenched hitch

I found Abraham's house situated in the center of the village on one of its half-mile long main streets. The house was noticeably smaller than the average, and its plywood siding was grayed and weather-etched—showing the effects of years of Alaska's harsh winds, snow and rain without a lick of paint. His house seemed consistent with Abraham and Eileen's pre-2005 lifestyle.

Community Awareness

If Abraham's story were true, there were several specific facts which I expected to find in Manokotak.

> **First**, that in a village of only 450, most if not all of its residents would definitely be aware of his accident and sensational story.

> **Second**, that I would be able to verify Ipli's claims of formerly being the nefarious town drunk, and that he had since 2006 been demonstrating a phenomenal life-transformation.

> **Third**, that I would find substantial proof of Abraham's positive Christian influence on the village.

> **Fourth**, that his testimony would most likely be controversial.

> And **fifth**, that I wouldn't find any evidence contradicting his testimony.

During my three-day stay in Manokotak, I discovered an array of positive evidence corroborating Abraham's claims and nothing to cause me to doubt its genuineness.

Testimonies of Abraham's Transformed Life

EILEEN GEORGE
Abraham's wife of 25 years said: *"He's a new man!"*

I stayed at the George's home for the three days I was in Manokotak. I met Abraham's children and wife, Eileen, but unfortunately I was unable to engage her in an interview because of her busyness with the affairs of the Spiritual Feast. I learned, however, that she had completely rejected Abraham's testimony for nearly two years but by 2007 had become a strong believer and advocate of her husband's testimony. In Chapter 10—"Three Key Witnesses"—there are many direct quotations and details of Eileen's personal journey to belief as well as her own story of transformation.

KARLA GEORGE
Abraham George's 24-year-old daughter shared the following observation: *"Dad has changed a lot. Dad has more love for us. Dad is around more and is more caring. Now Mom and Dad pray together and my dad prays for other people too."*

Testimony of Manokotak's Community Leaders

ARLENE FRANKLIN
Tribal Council Administrator and 30-year resident of Manokotak shared her observations: *"Abraham has changed very much since the accident."*

KEN NUKWAK
President of Manokotak Natives Limited Corporation and lifetime resident of Manokotak affirmed: *"He [Abraham] showed me that people **can** sober up. Other people sobered up who were willing to listen to his message. He has had influence on the young people."*

SALLY NUKWAK
Community Health Aide and longtime neighbor of the George's said: *"At first I didn't believe it when his mother-in-law said that he had changed, after hearing his testimony at his house. She was smiling and told me that I will like his testimony when I hear it. People were skeptical that he changed, thinking he'd go back to drinking again, but no! He started traveling to villages soon after... Nowadays, we consider Ipli and Eileen our brother and sister in Christ."*

MELVIN ANDREW
Former VPSO and current mayor of Manokotak: *"By November 2006 Abraham George became a new person to me. I am totally convinced that Abraham has had a true visitation from our Lord Jesus Christ and was given a task to tell His children a message. My life has changed because of what Jesus Christ did for Abraham. Abraham is now my best friend and co-worker in 'harvesting' souls for Jesus. I traveled with him on three*

occasions and clearly this man was true to what he was saying... Abraham is genuine and truthful in his testimony... The 'town reject' became a 'rejoice for the Lord!'[4]

Melvin and Sally Andrew

ABRAHAM ELECTED TO VILLAGE LEADERSHIP

Within a year after returning to Manokotak, Abraham had experienced something he had never known before—credibility and recognition. His past deeds had been forgiven and seemingly nearly forgotten. In 2006 Abraham was elected to the office of "Elder" in the Moravian Church

4   *See also Chapter 10, "Three Key Witnesses", for more of Melvin's credentials and testimony.*

and faithfully served in that capacity for three years. In 2008, he was also elected to serve on the Village Council.

This public recognition occurred in spite of Abraham's repeated self-renunciation of any personal credit for any of the many phenomenal accomplishments which had taken place at his hand. Abraham frequently declared publicly: *"Everything that's happening is not from me—I don't claim it. It's the Lord."*

> *"By December 2006, Abraham George was elected by Manokotak's Moravian Congregation as Elder... and was later elected to the local Village Council."*
>
> ~MELVIN ANDREW

> *"Abraham George is an active serving elder of the Manokotak Moravian Church. Ipli has the support of his pastor, local church board, collaboration of the traditional elders in the community, and encouragement of the local VPSO, as well as many other notable people in the community."*
>
> ~BISHOP WILLIAM NICHOLSON

These two appointments by village leaders constituted the highest possible public recognition of Abraham's newly found moral character and integrity. Their selection also clearly revealed a consensus of agreement with his testimony claims, for surely they would not have appointed a suspected public fraud.

These two appointments to public office by his home community are of inestimable apologetic value. All the leaders appointing Abraham were clearly aware of his reprehensible past, his horrendous accident and remarkable recovery, and had ample time and opportunity to observe his lifestyle since his return to the village in January 2006. The value and weight of the evidence provided by their **unified convictions** expressed by their votes, could never be duplicated by investigation, research or interviews. Clearly their votes boldly declared with confidence their unified convictions that Abraham was telling the truth.

THE WIND IS BLOWING.

POSITIVE EVIDENCE FROM ABRAHAM'S NEGATIVE NEIGHBORS

While in Manokotak, I was able to interview two of Abraham's staunchest religious adversaries. I considered this an extraordinary opportunity because I reasoned that, if any discrediting evidence of Abraham or his testimony existed in Manokotak, surely these guys would be aware of it and glad to divulge it to me.

When I arrived for the interview, the man answering the door had dark penetrating eyes that made me nervous. His face displayed deeply furrowed frown marks and not a hint of a smile. His demeanor was guarded and cold. I introduced myself, saying I was in Manokotak on a fact-finding mission regarding Abraham George. I told them that I had heard that they might have some definite opinions about Abraham and was hoping they would be willing to share with me anything they knew about him.

The first one to speak opened with a curt religious declaration: *"We are pure Moravians—**pure** Moravians!"* Then I asked what specifically their contention with Abraham was? It became immediately apparent that they were both upset over a new spontaneous worship style which they were convinced had been introduced into their church liturgy by Abraham and his followers. Seemingly, that was all they wanted to talk about, because that's all they did talk about.

I re-asked the same question a couple more times in a couple of different ways and their answers always reverted back to the liturgy issue. My closing question was intended to put a squeeze on their religious minds in an attempt to ferret out anything negative they might be harboring. I asked, *"If someone were to ask you whether Abraham's testimony was from God or the devil, what would your answer be?"* The room grew silent. I waited and re-asked the same question. I waited another **long two minutes** for a response. Neither of them would say anything.

I thanked them for their time and left. From their silence, I deduced that neither of them wanted to go on record acknowledging Abraham George's story as being from God, nor were they brazen enough to attribute all the good Abrahamic happenings they had no doubt been hearing about, to the devil. From what they didn't say, I felt I had gained a real testimonial trophy—that in Manokotak, incriminating evidence must not exist. The truth of this conclusion was soon reinforced by Ken Nukwak, a well-respected lifetime resident of Manokotak, who confidently affirmed: *"There is no evidence that it **didn't** happen."*

THE PROOF OF THE TRANSFORMATION OF MANOKOTAK

THE STATE OF MANOKOTAK BEFORE 2005

The following depiction of Manokotak prior to 2005, was given by state law enforcement officer Melvin Andrew: *"Manokotak was known to be riddled with alcohol-related criminal activity and it became the norm to expect criminal activity on weekends throughout the winter travel season [when snowmobile travel was possible]. On average I would have five alcohol-related incidents in one weekend. This number would increase after fishing and during the winter. Domestic violence was incredibly high also."*

THE POSITIVE IMPACT OF ABRAHAM'S TESTIMONY
AND MINISTRY ON THE VILLAGE OF MANOKOTAK

Manokotak resident, Ken Nukwak, reported: *"Before Abraham's accident, everybody [in Manokotak] was fighting and there was a lot of drinking all over town... now there's some fighting, but not with alcohol. It's a lot better; almost gone away."*

Arlene Franklin, a 30-year resident of Manokotak and Tribal Council Administrator reported: *"Abraham's testimony touches a lot of people, young and old. He has led many people to Christ through his testimony and praying for them. I'm one of the people who have been touched by his testimony and don't want to live the way I used to live before. A lot of young people like me have changed. Probably over 50 young people have been changed and even married couples."*

Bishop William Nicholson made the following comment about Ipli's influence on the transformation of Manokotak: *"The most convincing proof I've encountered is the enormous impact of Abraham's message and ministry on the community of Manokotak. Its influence has fueled the Spiritual Feast movement, impacted countless lives, and positively affected nearly every area of life in the village."*

The following is an official report compiled by Manokotak village leaders, presenting the many notable positive changes they had observed in the community of Manokotak since 2006:

- A *decrease in crime and violence*.

- A *decrease in school related truancy and negative behavior* towards teachers and persons of authority.

Author's Note:
The VPSO supervisor questioned Melvin Andrew as to why no criminal reports had been submitted for a period of six months, following the 2007 Spiritual Feast.

- In 2011, Manokotak Nunaniq School was *recognized nationally* as a National Title I Distinguished School.

- An *increase in Bible study cell group participants,* where on one night a record of over 50 attended.

- An *increase* in the number of unwed couples who are choosing to get married.

- An *increased number of church members* traveling on Gospel outreach and evangelism to other communities.

- An *increased church attendance* from those accepting Jesus Christ and those renewing their relationship with Him."

(The above statistics have been taken directly from the report, which was prepared in 2012 to submit to the International Moravian leadership.)

It is very clear from the above evidence that Manokotak has been dramatically impacted by Abraham George since his return to the village in 2006. The question that begs answering now is what can account for these powerful and positive changes in the community, which have been documented here?

THE WIND IS BLOWING.

Chapter 13

THE FIVE INHERENT PROOFS WITHIN ABRAHAM'S TESTIMONY

PROOF 1: PROPHETIC "FORETELLING"

The proof of this argument is based on the premise that only God can accurately predict the future. Within Abraham's testimony there are several futuristic statements he made concerning himself and the State of Alaska, which over the past several years have all come to pass. Their fulfillment strongly supports the truth of Abraham's testimony and that its content is beyond his own invention.

The **first** of these impressive prophetic statements was: *"I will be with you and everywhere you go, my Holy Spirit will be with you and my power will be with you."* When I first heard Abraham make this incredulous statement in 2008, I decided to check out his story, thinking within myself, *"This will definitely be easy to disprove, because I am certain that 'drunks' don't go around demonstrating the power of the Holy Spirit!"* I truly believed I would be able to quickly disprove that claim and with it the whole preposterous story. I was wrong! I was shocked when I soon discovered that wherever Abraham had gone, the presence and power of the Holy Spirit **had** manifestly been with him. It seemed like the supernatural followed Ipli like a shadow. Melvin Andrew, one of several reliable eyewitnesses of this phenomenon affirmed: *"Abraham George prayed for the sick and they were healed. Abraham George prayed for the* *hurting and they became whole. Abraham George prayed for many to believe and many accepted Christ as their personal Lord and Savior."* The preceding chapters have presented many incidents of this promise being fulfilled.

THE WIND IS BLOWING.

The **second** prophetic statement is: *"You will be going to places you never even thought of going."* When considering the fact that in 2005, when Abraham fist made this statement, he was a "nobody from nowhere", he had a "minus" credibility factor, his integrity was bankrupt, his wife and others hated him and wanted him to die, his only reputation was being the "town drunk" in Manokotak and Dillingham, he was a habitual criminal that had a police record a mile long—it would have been unusual for Abraham to even be *"allowed"* in villages outside of Manokotak. What has actually taken place, though, seems incomprehensible—because he has been **invited by village leaders** to **over 78** villages, and the three largest cities in Alaska, to present his testimony. This poses two enigmatic questions. The first being: how could Abraham have predicted his own future? The second: how could he, by his own initiative and efforts, have gained such recognition and credibility so quickly in order to have been invited to so many places he had never been before, nor had he even *"thought of going"*, all over Alaska? The simplest answer to both questions and the most reasonable is the one Abraham himself gave—he was told before the fact by the One who alone knows the future—Jesus Christ, Himself.

The **third** remarkable prophetic statement Abraham made was: *"You will have friends that have my Spirit in them."* Before 2005, Abraham's closest friends were a handful of criminals, drug addicts, and drunks. The two buddies who accompanied him on the day of his fateful wood gathering trip are currently serving long prison sentences. I've learned over the past few years that now Abraham truly does have many Spirit-filled friends today—his wife, numerous pastors, and believers from all over the State of Alaska—and I'm proud to say that I have become one of them.

Abraham and Author on charter fishing boat

This poses another enigmatic question—how could this confounding accomplishment possibly be explained naturally? It certainly couldn't be attributed to Abraham's charismatic personality, his outstanding reputation, his impressive education, or his wealth. **What** then? Again I would strongly suggest that the simplest and most sensible answer is the one Abraham gave—he was told before the fact by Jesus himself that it was divinely predestined to happen.

THE WIND IS BLOWING.

The **fourth**—"You'll be persecuted." Abraham's foretold persecution began the moment he arrived home from his hospitalization in Anchorage. It was then that his wife began her nearly two-year tirade of unrelenting mocking and cursing him privately and publicly.

"Even his wife was against what he did at first."

~SALLY NUKWAK

I can attest that Abraham has indeed suffered the pain of rejection, criticism, castigation, and false accusations from family, church leaders, community leaders, relatives and neighbors.

Within a short time after his traveling ministry began, he came under severe attack by the Moravian denominational leaders, who for several years strove to discredit Abraham and shut down his ministry in Alaska.

In their assault they officially denounced him as *"a false teacher and the antichrist,"* and finally even excommunicated him. After witnessing this malicious religious attack, Melvin Andrew was moved by Abraham's humble response saying: *"Abraham George was labeled a false prophet, yet he showed them no discontent, but forgiveness."*

In Manokotak one of his local adversaries poured sugar in the gas tank of his new 200 hp outboard which ruined it. On another occasion someone put sugar in the gas tank of his pickup truck. In several of the villages where Ipli traveled, he has encountered fierce resistance and false accusations.

The **fifth**, and by far the most far-reaching and impressively accurate prophetic statement, was given to Abraham while en route from heaven back to his body on earth. He stated: *"Then He [Jesus] showed me the whole State of Alaska.[1] He showed me little fires breaking out in the small places. 'What is this?' I said. He said that He's pouring out His Holy Spirit upon all places in these last days. There will be revival."* Abraham could not have imagined that he himself was destined to be the igniting spark of the many "little fires" of revival in his vision of Alaska. Abraham's connection with this revival was recognized and spoken of by Bishop Nicholson who stated: *"Manokotak had their own outpouring and I believe Abraham George was the sparkplug."*

The powerful and fast moving expansion of the revival spoken of in this prophecy is presented in detail in Chapter 8—"A Spreading Flame."

PROOF 2: CONSISTENCY

Consistency is a fundamental attribute of "truth", which by its very nature is **absolute**. Because of this, truth can never be self-contradictory. It is the immutable nature of truth that underlies the familiar court-room practice of "cross-examination," the purpose of which is to probe into statements to uncover any inconsistencies (untruths) within them.

The more details a statement contains, the more difficult it becomes to

---

1 ADDITIONAL PROPHETIC FOOD FOR THOUGHT: *For readers familiar with contemporary prophetic ministries, I have presented two remarkably similar prophecies regarding spiritual revival in Alaska in the Appendix.*

maintain consistency in retelling it, especially if the statement is **not true**. On the other hand, if a statement loaded with details holds up under intense cross-examination, its veracity is significantly enhanced.

Abraham's testimony contains literally dozens of specific details—names, places, dates, numbers, and even colors, all of which make it extremely vulnerable to inconsistencies if it were not true. Each time his detailed testimony is retold, the likelihood of making inconsistent statements also increases.

I have heard Abraham re-tell his testimony multiple times, in various locations and to a variety of audiences. Even though he has never used notes, the story-line and the details have never changed and I've never heard him make an inconsistent statement in presenting his testimony.

20 IMPROMPTU QUESTIONS

In the process of my research, while analyzing Abraham's testimony, I developed a list of "20 questions" which were based on specific statements he had made. Some of my questions were for clarification, others for additional knowledge and insight. After completing my list, I made an impromptu phone call to Abraham's home. When he answered I asked him if he would be willing to answer 20 questions which I had come up with from his testimony. I also asked if it would be okay for me to record our conversation for the sake of clarity and accuracy. He had no reservations whatsoever. I felt that his calm and confident response displayed sincere genuineness.

I have included one segment of that phone interview about "angels," to convey how the questioning was conducted.

> *"Abraham, you mentioned 'angels' several times in your description of heaven. I want to ask you a few questions about angels. First, were there many angels or few?"*
>
> Instantly he responded: *"There were many."*
>
> Then I asked: *"Did they all look alike or were they different?"*
>
> Without hesitation he answered: *"They were all different."*

I asked: *"How were they different?"*

He answered: *"Some were huge and some more like human-size. Some had wings and some didn't. Some had wings like eagles and some like swans."*

I was very favorably impressed by the results of that phone interview, not only because of the consistency of his detailed answers, but even more so because his answers were quick and spontaneous. I was struck by Abraham's impressive ability to rattle off detailed answers to my probing questions about celestial reality—his answers flowed out of him, as though he were reliving his answers.

There is yet one other aspect of consistency which Abraham has continually demonstrated—that is his lifestyle and the obvious urgency with which he has conducted his ministry. I have observed that his life and ministry have been consistent with the urgent content of his testimony. In short, his testimony and his lifestyle are consistent. As I've said earlier, I have never met anyone more focused and urgent in their actions than Abraham George has been and continues to be even today.

PROOF 3: THE INTRINSIC POWER OF HIS TESTIMONY

I have observed that Abraham's testimony has frequently demonstrated an uncanny intrinsic power to effect dramatic changes in people's lives. This phenomenon has been reported by many people from many places who have either experienced it themselves or witnessed it in others.

For example, I recently received a phone call from a native woman in the Yukon Territory who was searching for more of Abraham's DVDs to send to her relatives. Her interest had been spurred because she had witnessed people in her town receive healings and salvation as a result of watching it.

The following quotation from a personal letter to Abraham is another example of this remarkable phenomenon. The letter is from a couple who live in Fairbanks, Alaska. They wrote:

"Ipli, my wife and I would like to thank you for bringing me to

Jesus. We saw your testimony on August 8, 2010, and I was brought to Jesus that day. God bless you!"

~D. AND L. PURVIS

I recently accompanied Abraham to the Anchorage Rescue Mission where he had been asked to give his testimony. In my opinion, his delivery was one of his worst I had ever witnessed. It was badly disorganized and out of time sequence. I would have given him a "C-" on his presentation. However, when he concluded, I was stunned when eight weeping men arose from their seats, walked to the front and knelt down, asking Abraham to pray for them to be forgiven of their sins and delivered from their addictions. That experience was a real eye-opener and confirmed to me that the message itself carries life-transforming power which definitely doesn't depend on the quality or the order of its delivery. Melvin Andrew has also observed this phenomenon and testified: *"His testimony still has a great impact today for those who accept it and those who don't."*

THE WIND IS BLOWING.

PROOF 4: THE TEST OF TIME—"TIME WILL TELL"

Sixty-eight years of life-experience have taught me that "time" is not, after all, the "healer all things," but it does seem to come very close to being the "revealer of all things." The **"test of time"** has proven to be an effective and trustworthy revealer of character, hypocrisy, lies and an effective verifier of truth. Life is lived forward in time, but life's lessons are learned by looking back in time. Time has the unique capability of wearing away the veneer of hypocrisy and pretense and exposing the truth.

In 2006, when Abraham presented his testimony for the first time to his home village, he concluded his message by throwing down a logical and propositional challenge by which all would eventually be able to determine whether his claims were true or not. His argument was based on the "test of time"—*"If this [everything contained in his testimony] is from God, it will last. If it's not, it will not last."*

Nine years have now passed since Abraham made that bold challenge. The verdict of the nearly 10-year test of time is that Abraham has stayed out of jail, remained drug and alcohol free, stayed married to his one and only wife, has become a loving father to his children, a productive citizen and has been faithfully traveling and passionately telling the same story of heaven and hell over and over. I am unaware of any verifiable accusation of inconsistency or contradiction in his testimony or his life. Abraham and his testimony have successfully passed the test of time and it has told the truth!

THE WIND IS BLOWING.

PROOF 5: THE MANNER OF PRESENTATION OF HIS TESTIMONY—"TO SEE IT IS TO BELIEVE IT"

We have all heard the saying: **"To see it is to believe it."** I believe this cliché is especially fitting when it comes to Abraham's testimony. The first time I experienced (saw and heard) his testimony, I was very impressed by the manner of his presentation. He spoke with undeniable conviction and authority and at the same time displayed an unpretentious innocence. His body language and countenance strongly conveyed genuineness. Deep inside, I felt confirmation that Abraham was recounting an event which he had experienced, not telling a story. I couldn't imagine anyone lying that convincingly. Bishop Nicholson was also strongly impacted by the manner of his presentation. Following his first experience of hearing Ipli's testimony, he made the following observation: *"What struck me as Ipli opened his mouth was his utter sincerity and his humility. The greatest miracle, I felt, was Ipli standing up before the people and telling his story. Inside my spirit, I felt confirmation."*

This argument gains even more strength when realizing that Abraham's presentations have all been made in English, his second language, even though all of his celestial experiences and conversations took place in his native Yup'ik language. Further, Abraham had no training or experience in public speaking prior to being thrown into his public ministry. It's no wonder his eyes were clenched shut at the beginning of his public presentations.

138

In spite of all these factors, I found his presentation to be riveting and convincing. It made a deep impression on me—one that has never left. It was the manner in which he told his story that initially caught my attention and stirred my interest in proceeding into further investigation, ultimately resulting in the writing of this book.

I highly recommend experiencing his testimony for yourself—the same one that I did in February of 2008. It is still the most convincing presentation I've seen to date. It's available on the web at: **www. celestialtraveler.org**.

Chapter 14
STRANGE OCCURRENCES
THE CHAPTER I DIDN'T WANT TO WRITE

When the events described in this chapter were first related to me by Abraham, they struck me as being so bizarre that I determined to ignore them because I felt that including them could possibly diminish the credibility of the rest of the book. My reluctant reversal to include them occurred because I ultimately concluded that, though incredible, they were an integral part of Abraham's story and the evidence for them demanded their inclusion.

A FRIENDSHIP MADE IN HEAVEN

The phenomenon which I've come to refer to as the "Abraham-Everett connection," has been intellectually challenging and difficult to comprehend and express.

The "Abraham-Everett connection" is arguably as much Everett Blatchford's story as it is Abraham George's. Therefore, I have included basic biographical facts about Everett Blatchford and his special celestial experiences before describing his unfathomable and mysterious connection with Abraham George.

Everett Blatchford, now deceased, was 57 years old when he became a character in Abraham's dramatic and unfolding story. Everett, like Abraham, was also an Alaskan native (Yup'ik and Inupiat Eskimo). In

1983 he moved with his family to Nikiski, Alaska—a town of about 5,000, located on the famous Kenai Peninsula. Everett worked as a welder on the Alaska oil pipeline on the "North Slope."[1] Before his spectacular out-of-body experience in 2007, Everett was a backslidden Christian with negligible interest in spiritual things and seldom darkened the doors of a church.

EVERETT BLATCHFORD'S
NEAR-DEATH, LIFE-CHANGING EXPERIENCE

In 2007, while visiting his aunt in Seward, Alaska, Everett fell and struck his head on a concrete step. As a result of his head injury he was taken by ambulance to the Seward hospital where he "flat-lined"[2] several times. During one of those flat-line incidents he had an "out-of-body experience" which, incredibly, in every detail was nearly identical to Abraham George's.

After Everett returned to his body, he, like Abraham, immediately began telling everyone that he had met Jesus face-to-face and that he had been personally escorted by Him to hell and to heaven and back. He also received the identical three-fold message which had been given Abraham George—that *"Jesus is the way the truth and the life and no one comes to the Father but by him; that Jesus is coming soon; and that heaven and hell are realities."* Everett said he was sternly charged to tell this urgent message to all.

Upon returning home from his hospitalization in Seward, he, like Abraham, also demonstrated an immediate and radical lifestyle change. He passionately began telling about his extraordinary celestial experiences to anyone who would listen. According to Gus Flensburg *(Nikiski, Alaska)*, long-time friend of Everett's, *"After the Seward event there were phenomenal changes… He [Everett] was on a mission… He was driven and he told me that he had called every church in the area… Everett has had a great impact on my life".*

---

1   *The "North Slope" is a household word among Alaskans and refers to the northern coastal area of Alaska, rich in oil and natural gas: so-called because it is north of the Brooks Range extending down to the Arctic Ocean.*

2   *DEFINITION: (Medicine) to die or be so near death that the display of one's vital signs on medical monitoring equipment shows a flat line rather than peaks and troughs. (www.thefreedictionary.com/flatlined)*

Everett's grown son, Quincy Blatchford *(Kenai, Alaska)*, said: *"When my dad came back, he was hyper-spiritual and was always telling and warning anybody and everybody about Jesus and his experiences. Then he even started going out to the villages"*.

Abraham and Everett both confidently affirmed that while they were in heaven, they had an indescribable vision or dream-like spiritual encounter with each other. Both men also claimed to have been told that in the future (after returning to their bodies), they would meet again and would become intimate friends who would travel and minister together in the power of the Holy Spirit. Concerning this promise, Abraham said: *"When Jesus told me He was bringing me back to my body, He told me that I would be meeting a man who had a similar experience to mine."*

In October of 2007, Abraham and Everett, unbeknownst to each other, had both received and accepted invitations to share their testimonies at a special native spiritual gathering in Dillingham, Alaska.

During a community meal, a man sitting across the room from Abraham caught his eye. His gaze became transfixed as he tried to recall where and when he had met this man before. He felt drawn toward him. When Everett's eyes met his—they both, in a flash—recognized each other as that person they had met previously in heaven. They were both dumbfounded and ecstatic! They quickly moved toward each other and embraced jubilantly. Abraham recalled that breathtaking moment as follows: *"When I actually met him [Everett] in Dillingham, my dream played every detail. He [Everett] came for the gathering and he said that his dream was the same."* Abraham and Everett hugged each other as long-lost friends. Their friendship was spontaneous and electrical. Abraham described that encounter as: *"Everything was just like a magnet!"*

They had lots to talk about for sure. The "Abraham-Everett connection" which took on flesh in Dillingham, was to become the launch site for many powerful and productive joint ministry outreaches together. Abraham said: *"We went many places together—Barrow, Aleknagik, Fairbanks, Minto, Tetlin, and Northway."* Whenever and wherever they ministered together there was always a powerful, manifest-presence of the Holy Spirit, with many healing miracles and salvations.

Their relationship became exactly what Abraham had been foretold it would be. Everett's grown son, Quincy, described it as: *"an instant, intimate, and a strong bond."*

In addition to their many powerful ministry experiences together, there was also an uncanny recurring phenomenon between Abraham and Everett with telephone calls. This has been related by several sources. Everett's good friend, Gus Flensburg, spoke about it as follows: *"Whenever they [Abraham and Everett] called each other, one would call and the other one would be picking up the phone at the same time to receive the call... they'd just pick it up and start talking."* Everett's son, Quincy, also observed it and spoke of it saying: *"When my dad was going to call Abraham George, he would say: 'Watch this.' Then he picked up the phone and Abraham was there."*

Their friendship flourished until Everett's second and final death from pancreatic cancer in October of 2008. When that occurred, Abraham traveled several hundred miles to attend Everett's funeral. Ipli later named his first grandson "Everett" in honor of his beloved friend.[3]

Author's Note: For those of you who may be curious about the meaning and purpose of Everett's experience and how it relates to Abraham's, I have thought long and hard about it and I offer the following as my take on it. I have become convinced that Everett's experience was primarily for the purpose of confirming Abraham's experience as a second witness. My reasoning for this conclusion is based on two facts:

First, that relatively few doors ever opened for Everett Blatchford to share his equally amazing testimony and virtually hundreds of doors have opened for Abraham. Second, is the incomprehensible fact that not a single record (written or recorded) of Everett's testimony exists. I have tried many times in many ways to locate one, to no avail. On the other hand— for Abraham there are hundreds and possibly thousands of his DVDs in circulation far and wide.

It also served as a strong personal confirmation and encouragement to Abraham that his experience was real and not just a vision or dream. From what I have been able to determine, the only record which will remain of Everett Blatchford's celestial experience is what appears here in this book and in the memory of those he witnessed to.

---

3 *In Yup'ik tradition, it is common for grandparents to name their grandchildren.*

This *truly* was a *"friendship made in heaven"*.

A Plane Crash Averted By Angels

On February 17, 2010, Abraham and two of his native ministry partners boarded a Grant Air commuter airplane in Bethel, Alaska. They were heading for the village of Chefornak, where Abraham had been invited to speak and minister. It was going to be a routine 90-mile flight—or so they thought. That flight, they would soon learn, was going to be anything but "routine."

The Cessna 208 taxied down the runway. The takeoff was smooth and flawless. Within a half-hour the commuter plane made a scheduled en route stopover at the village of Kwigillingok to drop off two passengers and pick up two new ones.

The following is Abraham's account of what happened next:

"We were taking off [from Kwigillingok], and when the plane reached about 300 feet, it started sinking and then went down. It was like the power wasn't there, even though it was full throttle. When we took off, the plane had power, but somehow it started losing power as we went up. The wings started shuddering and the plane kept sinking until it hit the frozen tundra hard. It hit so hard, I thought the landing gear was going to split. Somehow the tires didn't blow out. The plane bounced and on the second bounce the plane hit on its right side wing which bent the wing upwards. Then the plane bounced again on the pond ice. I was praying and I shouted the name of 'Jesus' each time the plane hit the ground and every time the plane went up in the air and started taking off. I received a strong warning inside—for the pilot—which I knew was from the Lord. I told the pilot to 'not attempt to turn around or to land the plane, but to keep going straight ahead to the next village, to go full throttle and land full throttle'—and that's what he did. At that moment an angel appeared in the co-pilot seat next to the pilot. I started rubbing my eyes to make sure I was seeing right. His face was glowing and he had a big smile. He was

looking right at me, eye to eye. He had on white garments. I then looked out my window and I saw another angel under the right wing [the last 5 feet of which was now bent at 20 degrees]. It looked like he was holding it up with his fingertips. I looked out the left side window and I saw another angel under the left wing. I felt zero fear—just happiness. My spirit inside got so warm, I felt secure and at peace—like being held in God's hand—there's no way to describe how I felt. The people traveling with me on the plane were praying in the Spirit and they felt peace also.

When we got to Koliganek, we landed safely and all eight of us were unhurt. I said: 'Praise the Lord!' I then prayed for the pilot and he said: 'This shouldn't have happened with the wing in this condition; this plane shouldn't have taken off again.' When we landed at Koliganek there were planes and troopers[4] near the runway. We never made it to Chefornak."

TESTIMONY OF MOSES AYOJIAK, PASSENGER ON PLANE

Moses Ayojiak *(Togiak, Alaska)*, a ministry partner of Abraham, was with him on that fateful Feb. 17, 2010, Grant Air flight. He shared his recollections of that his experience as follows:

"I was with Ipli on the airplane and also Peter Jacob. I was sitting on the right side. There were eight of us in the plane.

*The weather wasn't good—kind of gray—so our plane was getting ice on the wing and it started swerving side to side. We tried to climb up but the plane went down and we hit the ground three times. The first time we hit the ground it was really hard, with the wheels. The second time we hit on the right wing—it was **loud**! Then I heard Ipli shout: 'JESUS!' The third time we hit the ground is when Ipli shouted, 'Jesus' really loud! And then we were starting to go. Ipli told the pilot 'not to turn back. Keep going straight'. On the way it seemed like something was—I felt it—holding our plane on the belly of the plane. Me and Ipli and Peter Jacob were worshipping God all the way. I was never afraid.*

"When we got to the ramp everybody was looking at our plane

---

4 *A team of Alaska State Troopers had flown into Koliganek earlier to investigate a recent murder case.*

and shaking their heads and saying: 'It's amazing'—these guys kept saying, 'It's amazing! It's a miracle!' People kept saying, 'It's a miracle!' The pilots [Earl and the plane's pilot] said, 'It's a miracle!'"

TESTIMONY OF JACOB PETER, PASSENGER ON PLANE

Jacob Peter *(Bethel, Alaska)* was another companion of Abraham on the Grant Air flight. He shared his recollections of that event as follows:

"Abraham was seated behind the pilot. I was praying in the Spirit the whole time, so I wasn't very aware of what was going on. I felt no fear—only peace and comfort. I heard him [Abraham] say 'Jesus!' but it sounded like he was far away. The second time he said 'Jesus!' it was louder. The third time it was very loud! I heard Abraham say to the pilot, 'Don't turn back! Fly to the next village.'

"When the pilot started slowing down the plane to land, the plane started moving from side to side like it was going to stall. Abraham said: 'Land full throttle!' After we were on the ground we stayed in the plane about a half an hour. I saw people outside looking at the plane and they were shaking their heads."

TESTIMONY OF EARL SAMUELSON, ALASKA STATE TROOPER PILOT

Earl Samuelson *(Napaskiak, Alaska)*, a 30 year veteran pilot for the Alaska State Troopers, happened to be on location at the Koliganek airport landing strip at the moment the crippled Cessna airplane hit the runway at full-throttle to land. Earl was there because he had flown in a team of state troopers to investigate a recent homicide. He personally witnessed the abnormally fast landing of the crippled plane. The following is Mr. Samuelson's account of what he witnessed:

Earl Samuelson: 30-year veteran pilot for the Alaska State Troopers.

"I saw the landing—the engine was under a lot of power. The landing was hard and flat, [as opposed to the normal soft and gradual] and

*it hit twice. When I saw the damaged condition of the plane's wing, I asked the pilot, 'How did you keep it in the air?' His answer was: 'I had a planeload of priests [Abraham and his travel companions] and they said they saw angels.' I said: **'I can believe it!'** With the wing bent as it was, **the plane should have rolled and crashed.** I grew curious, so I looked at the underside of the damaged wing. I noticed strange smudged fingerprints in the layer of exhaust soot under the damaged area of the wing. They weren't whole handprints, but only fingertip prints, which seemed odd.*

"*I took pictures of them on my cell phone. I made a call to Grant Air in Bethel and asked if they had worked on that wing recently. They said 'No'. I asked the same question to the pilot and got the same answer. In my opinion, those passengers are living miracles.*"

Earl Samuelson, out of his own personal curiosity, eliminated the two most likely natural explanations for the fingertip prints under the wing. Could these have been confirmation of what Ipli saw—angel fingertip prints? Below is the picture Earl Samuelson took of the fingertip prints.

THE WIND IS BLOWING.

Bent wing on crippled Cessna plane; a 20% bend, making it un-flyable.

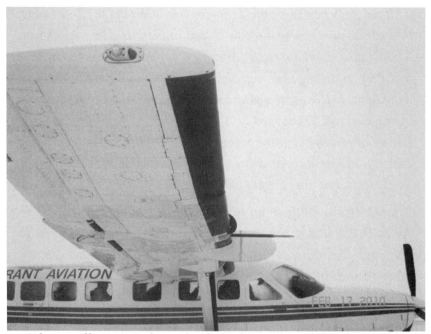

Side view of bent wing; photo taken by Earl Samuelson at Koliganek Airport immediately following emergency landing with Abraham and companions still on board—ALIVE!

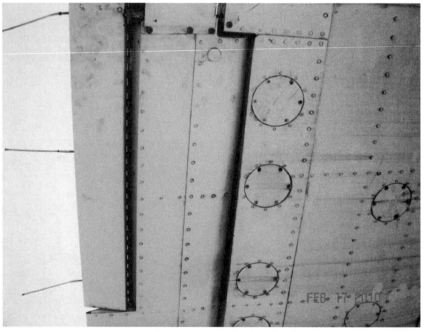

Mysterious fingerprints under the plane's wing

THE OFFICIAL FAA REPORT OF THIS ACCIDENT:

"On February 17, 2010, at 1657, Alaska standard time, a Cessna 208B, sustained substantial damage during impact with terrain following takeoff from the airport in Kwigillingok, Alaska. The airline transport pilot and his seven passengers were not injured. Grant Aviation, Anchorage, Alaska, was operating the aircraft. The intended destination was Kipnuk, Alaska. The pilot said that the takeoff was normal, but at 200 feet above the ground and in a turn, he observed a reduction in power. He moved the emergency fuel control lever forward, and power was restored. Before the sink rate could be reversed, the airplane impacted the surface of a frozen lake, and 5 feet of the outward right wing was bent upwards. The aileron was not damaged. The pilot stated that 'for safety reasons' he chose to fly straight ahead for 8 miles to Koliganek, Alaska, where the flight landed without further difficulty. The operator's maintenance personnel inspected the engine and airframe, and determined that the right wing required major repair to restore it to airworthy condition." [5]

Author's Note:
Regarding the pilot's statement: "for safety reasons." Does it make rational sense that after his plane had suffered severe damage to its wing that the "safest" way to safety would be to fly to a landing strip eight miles away, rather than to get the plane and its passengers on the ground as soon as possible at the airport at hand? I can truly empathize with the pilot not wanting to report to the FAA that a passenger sitting behind him—Abraham George—had instructed him to: "not attempt to turn around or to land the plane, but to keep going straight ahead full throttle to Koliganek!" This would be especially true if the pilot also included that the same passenger also reported seeing an "angel in the copilot seat and one under each wing." No wonder I could never get that pilot to talk to me!

---

5   Source: *National Transportation Safety Board–Official Factual Aviation Report. A photocopy of the official NTSB Accident Report is provided in the Appendix.*

MIRACLE OR FLUKE?

Abraham George Stated:	Witnesses Stated:
We were taking off and when the plane reached about 300 feet, it started sinking and then went down…the plane kept sinking until it hit the frozen tundra hard. The plane bounced and on the second bounce the plane hit on its right-side wing which bent the wing upwards. Then the plane bounced again on the pond ice. I was praying and I shouted the name of Jesus each time the plane hit the ground—and every time the plane went up in the air and started taking off.	FAA—The pilot said that the takeoff was normal, but at 200 feet above the ground and in a turn, he observed a reduction in power. Before the sink rate could be reversed, the airplane impacted the surface of a frozen lake, and 5 feet of the outward right wing was bent upwards.
I received a strong warning inside for the pilot which I knew was from the Lord. I told the pilot to not attempt to turn around or to land the plane, but to keep going straight ahead to the next village, to go full throttle and land full throttle and that's what he did.	FAA—The pilot stated that 'for safety reasons' he chose to fly straight ahead for 8 miles to Koliganek, Alaska, where the flight landed without further difficulty.

PASSENGER—I heard Abraham say to the pilot: 'Don't turn back. Fly to the next village.' When the pilot started slowing down the plane to land, the plane started moving from side to side like it was going to stall. |
| I then looked out my window and I saw another angel under the right wing [the last 5 feet of which was now bent at 20 degrees]. It looked like he was **holding it up with his fingertips.** | TROOPER PILOT—I grew curious, so I looked at the underside of the damaged wing. I noticed strange smudged fingerprints in the layer of exhaust soot under the damaged area of the wing. They weren't whole handprints, but **only fingertip prints**, which seemed odd. |
| I told the pilot to not attempt to turn around or to land the plane, but to keep going straight ahead to the next village—to go full throttle and land full throttle—and that's what he did. | TROOPER PILOT—I saw the landing—the engine was under a lot of power. The landing was hard and flat, and it hit twice.

PASSENGER—Abraham said: 'Land full throttle!'

FAA—The operator's maintenance personnel inspected the engine and airframe, and determined that the right wing required major repair to restore it to airworthy condition. |

ABRAHAM GEORGE STATED:	WITNESSES STATED:
	TROOPER PILOT—When I saw the damaged condition of the plane's wing, I asked the pilot, 'How did you keep it in the air?' His answer was: 'I had a planeload of priests [Abraham and his travel companions] and they said they saw angels'. I said: 'I can believe it.' With the wing bent as it was, the plane should have rolled and crashed.
I then prayed for the pilot and he said: 'This shouldn't have happened with the wing in this condition; this plane shouldn't have taken off again.'	FAA—The airline transport pilot and his seven passengers were not injured.
	TROOPER PILOT—In my opinion, those passengers are living miracles. ~EARL SAMUELSON *NAPASKIAK, ALASKA*
	PASSENGER—When we got to the ramp... everybody was looking at our plane and shaking their heads and saying: 'It's amazing'—these guys keep saying, 'It's amazing! It's a miracle!' People kept saying, 'It's a miracle!' The pilots said, 'It's a miracle!'" ~MOSES AYOJIAK *TOGIAK, ALASKA*

TURNING WINE INTO WATER

The following bizarre incident was related to me by Henry Shavings, Jr., a longtime native resident of Manokotak and one of Ipli's earliest converts, who soon became a staunch advocate and traveling partner of Abraham's. Henry continues to be a committed and active participant in advancing the cause of Abraham George.

Henry delights in sharing the following unusual and humorous prayer of Abraham's which Henry personally overheard while traveling with him on one of their early village mission trips. With a grinning face he described it in the following way:

"On one of those traveling times, before Abraham's wife was converted, Abraham had been praying for his wife, Eileen—for God to 'turn her alcohol into water.' Then Eileen called her husband

saying: 'Ipli! Stop praying for me—I can't get drunk; my alcohol is like water!' Hee, hee, hee! God is good that he can change wine into water. I believe after that time Eileen converted and was saved due to her husband praying for her."

~HENRY SHAVINGS, JR.
MANOKOTAK

I believe that the three preceding mysterious incidents again demonstrate the supernatural nature of Abraham's life and ministry and constitute additional circumstantial proof of the promise he claims to have received from Jesus—*"I will be with you and My power will be with you."* This has been Abraham's only explanation of the supernatural presence in his ministry and I have yet to discover any other plausible explanation.

THE WIND IS BLOWING.

Chapter 15
THE PROOF OF
BIBLICAL CONFIRMATION

The Bible has more to say concerning the afterlife than any other book of antiquity. For countless millions, the Bible has been reverentially held to be the "Word of God" and for them the Bible has been considered to be an authoritative source of knowledge and insight into the spirit world and afterlife. For "Bible believers"—those whose beliefs have been formulated and foundationally anchored to the teachings of the Bible—it would be essential for the content of Abraham's testimony to be consistent and harmonious with biblical teaching in order to be accepted as genuine. This was the case for Ken Nukwak, a Bible-believing Christian from Manokotak, who came to acceptance of Abraham's testimony from personally comparing it with Bible teaching. Ken confessed: *"I believe his testimony because of the Bible."* For Bible believers like Mr. Nukwak, this chapter will likely be the most significant and convincing proof of all.

There are actually two lines of proof that can be derived from the Biblical content within Abraham's testimony in this chapter. The first is based solely on the prolific and accurate biblical content. The second is based on the incongruous extenuating factors involved in Abraham's presentation of it.

BIBLICAL CONTENT WITHIN ABRAHAM'S TESTIMONY

Abraham's testimony, though never quoting from the Bible, contains at least *52 statements* which accurately portray or allude to biblical teaching or are consistent with biblical concepts and precedents and simultaneously are free of overt contradictions with biblical teaching on death and the afterlife.

Author's Note: It is important to understand the definition of "contradiction" as used herein, which is: "The statement of a position opposite to one already made... a difference or disagreement between two things which means that both cannot be true" (Webster). In other words, if one statement is asserted to be true, then a contradictory statement cannot also be true.

Below is a comparison chart of statements from Abraham's testimony with corresponding biblical statements[1].

These are presented under the following seven categories:

(1) HEAVEN
(2) THE PERSONHOOD OF JESUS
(3) THE THRONE OF GOD
(4) THE ANGELS IN HEAVEN
(5) THE SOULS IN HEAVEN
(6) OUTER DARKNESS AND HELL
(7) GENERAL BIBLICAL REFERENCES

HEAVEN

ABRAHAM'S STATEMENT	BIBLICAL CORRELATION
This place is lit by God's glory... There was no sun and no shadows.	The city does not need the sun or the moon to shine on it, for the glory of God gives it light, and the Lamb is its lamp. —Revelation 21:23
That place was full of bright smoke like a bright fog around the throne—real powerful smoke.	...the doorposts and thresholds shook and the temple was filled with smoke. —Isaiah 6:4
Seems like bright fog was moving on and in her garments. [speaking of seeing Balakea John; pg. 41]	The one who is victorious will be dressed in white. —Revelation 3:5
	...a great multitude wearing white robes —Revelation 7:9

---

1 All Bible quotations taken from the New International Version (NIV) unless otherwise indicated.

ABRAHAM'S STATEMENT	BIBLICAL CORRELATION
God's presence is everywhere and in everything.	Do not I fill heaven and earth? declares the Lord. —*Jeremiah 23:24*
	The heavens, even the highest heaven cannot contain you. —*I Kings 8:27*
These mansions were not made by human hands, but by the glory of God.	In My Father's house are many mansions —*John 14:2 (NEW KING JAMES VERSION)*
	...we have a building from God, an eternal house in heaven, not built by human hands. —*2 Corinthians 5:1*
The trees had mostly green leaves. Jesus told me: 'They are for the healing of the nations.'	And the leaves of the tree are for the healing of the nations. —*Revelation 22:2*
	...and their leaves for healing. —*Ezekiel 47:12*
Everything up in heaven moves whenever God is praised—even the grass and flowers move in harmony.	Let the fields be jubilant, and everything in them; let all the trees of the forest sing for joy. —*Psalm 96:12*
	...and all the trees of the field will clap their hands —*Isaiah 55:12*
	...if they keep quiet, the stones will cry out. —*Luke 19:40*
I saw twelve gates. There were three on each side. They looked like the inside of a clam only brighter.	It had a great high wall with 12 gates —*Revelation 21:12*
	The twelve gates were 12 pearls, each gate made of a single pearl. —*Revelation 21:21*
Then I saw golden streets that you could see right through.	The great street of the city was of gold, as pure as transparent glass. —*Revelation 21:21*
They were all different nationalities.	...persons from every tribe and language and people and nation. —*Revelation 5:9*
	...a great multitude from every nation, tribe, people and language —*Revelation 7:9*

Table continued →

Abraham's Statement	Biblical Correlation
'This river is from my Father's throne.'	...the river of the water of life, as clear as crystal, flowing from the throne of God and of the Lamb. —Revelation 22:1
He took me places—just like blinking of an eye.	...the Spirit of the Lord suddenly took Philip away... Philip, however appeared at Azotus —Acts 8:39-40

The Personhood of Jesus

Abraham's Statement	Biblical Correlation
I still couldn't see his face–it was too bright. He was a man figure but he was so full of light—he was so bright, I couldn't see his face; it was too bright.	...his face like lightning, his eyes like flaming torches —Daniel 10:6
	His face shone like the sun —Matthew 17:2
	...his face was like the sun shining in all its brilliance —Revelation 1:16
	...his face like lightning —Daniel 10:6
I felt love, joy, and peace from Him.	Jesus looked at him and loved him. —Mark 10:21
	Now Jesus loved Martha and her sister and Lazarus. —John 11:5
	The fruit of the Spirit is love —Galatians 5:22
I felt like a dirty rag—unworthy to be in His presence, I felt ashamed of my past and knew I had no right, as a sinner to stand before Him.	I am a man of unclean lips — Isaiah 6:4-6
	John answered them all, "I baptize you with water. But one who is more powerful than I will come, the straps of whose sandals I am not worthy to untie. He will baptize you with the Holy Spirit and fire." — Luke 3:16
	The centurion replied, "Lord, I do not deserve to have you come under my roof. But just say the word, and my servant will be healed." —Matthew 8:8

Abraham's Statement	Biblical Correlation
When I saw his hands I saw nail prints.	Then he said to Thomas, Put your finger here; see my hands. Reach out your hand and put it into my side. —*John 20:27*
Jesus told me: 'I know your every word before it comes out of your mouth.'	…you perceive my thoughts from afar. Before a word is on my tongue you, Lord, know it completely. —*Psalm 139:2, 4*
	The Lord knows the thoughts of man. —*Psalm 94:11 (NKJV)*
	Immediately Jesus knew in his spirit that this was what they were thinking in their hearts —*Mark 2:8*
We'll be like Jesus—when we see Him.	…when Christ appears, we shall be like him, for we shall see him as he is . —*1 John 3:2-3*
Jesus told me: 'Tell my children, I am the way, and the truth, and the life. No man comes to the Father but by me.'	Jesus answered, "I am the way and the truth and the life. No one comes to the Father except through me." —*John 14:6*
Everything happened at Jesus' command. He had enormous power. The power of Jesus is so awesome that nobody could imagine it here on earth. Every time when He spoke, it instantly happened.	What kind of man is this? Even the winds and the waves obey him! —*Matthew 8:27*
	All authority in heaven and on earth has been given to me. —*Matthew 28:18*
Jesus said to me, 'Tell my children I'm coming soon—sooner than they think!'	Look, I am coming soon! He who testifies to these things says, "Yes, I am coming soon." —*Revelation 22:7, 20*

THE THRONE OF GOD

ABRAHAM'S STATEMENT	BIBLICAL CORRELATION
Then I saw a glorious throne with a bright figure on it. From where I was standing the throne looked like it was about twelve feet high. That place was full of bright smoke like bright fog around the throne—real powerful smoke. I can't describe it with words.	...there before me was a throne in heaven And the one who sat there had the appearance of jasper and ruby. *—Revelation 4:2-3*
	I saw the Lord, high and exalted, seated on a throne and the temple was filled with smoke *—Isaiah 6:1, 4*
	And the temple was filled with smoke from the glory of God and from his power *—Revelation 15:8*
There were also all the colors of the rainbow, only they were keener than on earth.	A rainbow that shone like an emerald encircled the throne. *—Revelation 4:3*
I saw lightning and heard loud thunder. To me it was God the Father's glory.	From the throne came flashes of lightning, rumblings and peals of thunder *—Revelation 4:5*
Around the throne there were four huge angel-like beings—one posted on each corner. There was also one flying above the throne in a bright cloud—he was the loudest. They had many eyes and each had six wings—upper, middle, lower. The upper wings would cover their faces, lower wings would cover their feet, and with the middle wings they would fly up and down, worshiping. As one went up, another one would go down—nonstop. They would sing: 'Holy, holy, holy, Lord God Almighty!'	...I saw the Lord... seated on the throne... Above him were seraphim, each with six wings: With two wings they covered their faces, with two they covered their feet, and with two they were flying. And they were calling to one another: 'Holy, holy, holy is the Lord Almighty *—Isaiah 6:1–3*
	In the center, around the throne, were four living creatures, and they were covered with eyes, in front and in back. Each of the four living creatures had six wings and was covered with eyes all around... Day and night they never stop saying: 'Holy, holy, holy is the Lord God Almighty *—Revelation 4:6, 8*
Then he showed me this crystal clear river. The water was moving and glowing. I never saw in my whole life water as clear. Then I thought, 'Where does this river come from?' Jesus answered my thought: 'This river is from my Father's throne.'"	Then the angel showed me the river of the water of life, as clear as crystal, flowing from the throne of God and of the Lamb *—Revelation 22:1*

The Angels in Heaven

Abraham's Statement	Biblical Correlation
There were so many angels.	Then I looked, and heard the voice of many angels, numbering thousands upon thousands, and ten thousand times ten thousand. *—Revelation 5:11*
	You have come to thousands upon thousands of angels *—Hebrews 12:22*
The angels' singing was out of this world! They take turns when they sing. They sing this one verse and then the other angels sing the same verse.	And they were calling to one another: 'Holy, holy, holy is the Lord Almighty' *—Isaiah 6:3*
They were all different. Some had wings like swans, some like giant eagles.	...the fourth was like a flying eagle. *—Revelation 4:7*
I could see four big angels on earth's four corners.	I saw four angels standing at the four corners of the earth *—Revelation 7:1*

The Souls in Heaven

Abraham's Statement	Biblical Correlation
Everywhere I see these same souls were wearing white, white, white garments—seems like gowns.	They were dressed in white and had crowns of gold on their heads. *—Revelation 4:4*
	Then each of them was given a white robe *—Revelation 6:11*
I turned around and He showed me lots of little children—it looked like thousands of little children as far as my eyes could see.	Jesus said, "Let the little children come to me, and do not hinder them, for the kingdom of heaven belongs to such as these." *—Matthew 19:14*
	[King David said:] While the child was still alive, I fasted and wept. But now that he is dead, why should I go on fasting? Can I bring him back again? I will go to him, but he will not return to me. *—2 Samuel 12:18-23.*

Table continued →

Abraham's Statement	Biblical Correlation
Then He showed me my deceased relatives who were up there. He allowed me to see and talk with my late father, my grandparents, my great-grandparents, and my great-great-grandparents.	Isaac breathed his last and died and was gathered to his people *—Genesis 35:28-29*
	Jacob breathed his last and was gathered to his people. *—Genesis 49:33*
Even though some of my relatives died before I was born, I knew them and they knew me.	Now I know in part; then I shall know fully, even as I am fully known. *—Corinthians 13:12*

Outer Darkness and Hell

Abraham's Statement	Biblical Correlation
Jesus told me, 'This place is for the devil and his angels—not for my children.'	Depart from me you who are cursed, into the eternal fire prepared for the devil and his angels. *—Matthew 25:41*
On the third plea, Jesus would answer them. Everything was on three.	So he left them and went away once more and prayed the third time, saying the same thing. *—Matthew 26:44*
	Three times I pleaded with the Lord to take it away from me. *—2 Corinthians 12:8*
I wondered who these were and why they were there. Jesus said: 'These are the souls of the unprofitable servants and those that backslid.' I heard gnashing of teeth, wailing, crying and souls screaming!	Then the king said to the servants, 'Bind him hand and foot and cast him into outer darkness; there will be weeping and gnashing of teeth.' *—Matthew 22:13 (NKJV)*
	And throw that worthless servant outside, into the darkness, where there will be weeping and gnashing of teeth. *—Matthew 25:30*
	But the subjects of the kingdom will be thrown outside, into the darkness *—Matthew 8:12*
	…those who shrink back and are destroyed *—Hebrews 10:39*

160

Abraham's Statement	Biblical Correlation
Jesus said, 'I waited for you with outstretched arms and I was ready to forgive you. But you didn't come to me.'	All day long I have held out my hands to an obstinate people, who walk in ways not good… —Isaiah 65:2
	Come to Me, all you who labor and are heavy laden, and I will give you rest. —Matthew 11:28
I'm tired of being tormented… I'm thirsty… While you were on earth you lived in earthly pleasure.	'Father Abraham send Lazarus to dip the tip of his finger in water and cool my tongue, because I am in agony in this fire.' "But Abraham replied, 'Son, remember that in your lifetime you received your good things, while Lazarus received bad things, but now he is comforted here and you are in agony. —Luke 16:24-25
That place is dark but I saw the souls in the pits and they were covered with fire and worms. The fire was swirling around them but it didn't burn them up or the worms. The worms were in them and they were covered with worms—completely covered… All these vile worms were coming in and out from their eyes, nose, mouth and ears. The worms did not burn and did not die.	May burning coals fall upon them; may they be thrown into the fire, into miry pits, never to rise. —Psalm 140:10
	…those who rebelled against me; the worms that eat them will not die, the fire that burns them will not be quenched… —Isaiah 66:24
	…to go to hell, into the fire that shall never be quenched—where 'Their worm does not die And the fire is not quenched.' —Mark 9:43, 48 (NKJV)
	Anyone whose name was not found written in the book of life was thrown into the lake of fire. —Revelation 20:15
The first soul Jesus allowed me to see was this poor soul who was a drunk and didn't have faith in Him. When his life was over he ended up in hell.	Or do you not know that wrongdoers will not inherit the kingdom of God? Do not be deceived: Neither the sexually immoral nor idolaters nor adulterers nor men who have sex with men nor thieves nor the greedy nor drunkards nor slanderers nor swindlers will inherit the kingdom of God. —1 Corinthians 6:9,10

Table continued →

ABRAHAM'S STATEMENT	BIBLICAL CORRELATION
'I was in church most of my life. I was a minister while on earth. How come I'm here?' Jesus answered that poor soul and said: 'When you didn't care for that one least poor soul that nobody cared about; when you did that to him you did it to me. 'I was a stranger and you never accepted me. I was sick, you never came to me. I was hungry, you never fed me. I was in prison, you never came to me. When you didn't care for that one poor soul, you didn't care for me.' The one who thought he was a minister, at this time he is in hell.	Many will say to me on that day, 'Lord, Lord, did we not prophesy in your name, and in your name drive out demons and perform many miracles?' Then I will tell them plainly, 'I never knew you. Away from me, you evildoers!' —Matthew 7:22-23 '...whatever you did not do for one of the least of these, you did not do for me.' Then they will go away to eternal punishment, but the righteous to eternal life. —Matthew 25:45-46
Before you were born I knew you.	Before I formed you in the womb I knew you —Jeremiah 1:5 Before I was born the Lord called me... —Isaiah 49:1
Demons know Jesus and stay far from him.	In the synagogue there was a man possessed by a demon, an impure spirit. He cried out at the top of his voice, "Go away! What do you want with us, Jesus of Nazareth? Have you come to destroy us? I know who you are—the Holy One of God!" —Luke 4:33-34

GENERAL BIBLICAL REFERENCES

ABRAHAM'S STATEMENT	BIBLICAL CORRELATION
I'll be with you wherever you go.	And surely I am with you always, to the very end of the age. —Matthew 28:20 I will never leave you, nor forsake you." —Hebrews 13:5 (NKJV)

162

He's pouring out his Holy Spirit upon all these places in these last days.	I will pour out my Spirit on all people. Even on my servants, both men and women, I will pour out my Spirit in those days. —Joel 2:28-29
	Even on my servants, both men and women, I will pour out my Spirit in those days... —Acts 2:18

ABRAHAM'S STATEMENT	BIBLICAL CORRELATION
Abraham told Melvin one time that if he ever saw him in the woods he would kill him. They became the worst possible enemies. *"Abraham is now my best friend."* ~MELVIN ANDREW	...the Lord causes their enemies to make peace with them. —Proverbs 16:7
I was far from God.	But now in Christ Jesus you who once were far away have been brought near by the blood of Christ... —Ephesians 2:13
Abraham George was dreaded by Melvin and the Alaska State Troopers. On one of his arrests, he astonishingly ripped the handcuffs apart!	When Jesus got out of the boat, a man with an impure spirit came to meet him. This man lived in the tombs, and no one could bind him anymore, not even with a chain. For he had often been chained but he tore the chains apart. —Mark 5:2-4
Deep inside I felt He cared very much about me.	Cast all your anxiety on him because he cares for you. —1 Peter 5:7

Another substantial proof emerges from the prolific and accurate biblical content within Abraham's testimony—especially when considering the following facts of Abraham's background. By way of review these facts are re-presented here. **First,** he was biblically illiterate: *"I never read the Bible."* As a lifelong hard-core unbeliever he kept himself free from any biblical indoctrination. **Second,** Abraham's native language and all of the communications in his celestial experiences were in Yupik. Therefore everything given in his English language testimony had to be translated by him ad-lib. **Third,** Abraham never wrote any of his celestial conversations and experiences down, nor has he ever used written notes in presenting his testimony.

I confidently maintain that what Abraham has accomplished here would require the work of surpassing genius, and, naturally speaking, is beyond human possibility.

THE WIND IS BLOWING.

Chapter 16
WHY ABRAHAM GEORGE?

If you're at all like me, you've got to have wondered: "Why would a man as bad as Abraham George had been, be chosen for such a monumental and holy task?" At the beginning of this endeavor I was troubled and perplexed by this enigmatic question. From a purely legalistic/religious point of view, Abraham would seem to have been the least likely person on earth to be chosen for such a role. Throughout this undertaking I have been watching for clues in hope of satisfying this perplexing question for myself. I've been in the company of Mr. George now at various times and places for several years. I have all the while maintained a watchful eye and sensitive ear to learn all I can about this unique person. Along the journey I have discovered a number of interesting and pertinent facts about Abraham which have helped me understand why God may have chosen him. I have actually come to the conclusion that **Abraham was the perfect choice for his assignment.** Below are a few of the significant discoveries which have brought me to this conclusion.

PRAYER

The first and most obvious possibility is prayer. Just the prayers offered on his behalf—specifically mentioned in Abraham's testimony—are numerous, and one can only imagine that there were many others.

"The family thanked everyone who prayed for Abraham."
                                          ~MELVIN ANDREW

The first prayer specifically mentioned was Manokotak's local Pastor John Nicori, who, according to Melvin Andrew, *"arrived at the clinic and prayed for Abraham."* The second was an Orthodox priest, Father Peter Chris:

> *"When I came to [in Anchorage], he was praying for me. He anointed me with holy oil and prayed, 'Father if it is your will, extend his life'—he prayed this three times"*
>   ~ABRAHAM GEORGE[1]

The third was Doc Nicholson, who as chaplain was summoned to pray for Abraham while he was hospitalized. Finally, there were the fervent prayers of Mary, Abraham's mother who made daily visits to pray for him. If only one of those many prayers got through, it could account for some or all of Abraham's experience—*"The effective, fervent prayer of a righteous man avails much."* (James 5:16)

CHOSEN BY GOD TO DELIVER HIS MESSAGE

On one occasion I posed this question to Abraham himself: *"Have you ever wondered why God chose you to have been given another chance at life and such an awesome experience?"* He quickly gave a dual answer: *"Yes—I asked Jesus and He told me—'I chose you before I formed you in your mother's womb'"*—an obvious reference to the inscrutable and sovereign predestination of God. In the second part of his answer he said: *"Jesus knew what's going to happen after He brings me back to my body. He knew the future. His message is going to go to His children. He wants me to show His children and to tell His children that He is the Way, the Truth and the Life."* In his unique Yup'ik idiom Abraham was saying: *"Jesus chose me because He knew that **I would get the job done** of telling His message to everyone he would send me to."*

---

1   *This was what Don Piper experienced, who stated in his book, 90 Minutes in Heaven: "While I was in heaven, a Baptist preacher came on the accident scene. Even though he knew I was dead, he rushed to my lifeless body and prayed for me... At least 90 minutes after the EMTs pronounced me dead, God answered that man's prayers. I returned to earth." (Don Piper, 90 Minutes in Heaven)*

166

TENACITY AND ENDURANCE

"Abraham doesn't allow resistance to get him down. He is like a war horse with blinders!"

~KEN NUKWAK
NEIGHBOR WHO OBSERVED THIS TRAIT

Abraham's track record verifies that based on this criteria, he was definitely the right choice. He has, from the beginning, displayed a forehead of flint when it comes to tenacity and endurance. In one of my interviews of Ipli, he forewarned me: *"You're dealing with a stubborn Yup'ik man!"* Time has proven this statement. In spite of intense persecution and trials he has remained undeterred and undaunted. He has forged onward in spite of experiencing rejection, criticism, harassment, and false accusations.

From the moment he returned to his body in the Alaska Native Medical Center in 2005, Abraham began to fervently declare his heavenly experience and message to anyone who would listen. Since then Abraham has traveled in all seasons and in all types of weather by airplane, automobile, snow machine, ATV, and boat to over 78 villages and cities in Alaska and the Yukon, passionately declaring his story. In my 68 years, I have never met anyone more committed and intensely focused on their mission than him. Abraham's unique DNA of tenacity, commitment and fiery fervor has equipped him to finish his assignment, confirming him to be the perfect choice for the job.

"I know he won't quit spreading the gospel of Jesus, for he made a commitment to do so."

~SALLY NUKWAK

LARGE EXTENDED FAMILY

I have also discovered that Abraham was born into a huge extended family network which over the decades has been dispersed all across Alaska and into Canada. Abraham once told me: *"My dad had 15 brothers and sisters and his dad had 13 brothers and sisters born in the Yukon. In the late 1800's, seven of them moved to the Kuskokwim Delta in Western Alaska. I have relatives in more than 20 villages—even Barrow."* I have

167

never met anyone with more aunts, uncles, cousins, second cousins, nephews and nieces. This fact has served as a positive and practical aid in Abraham's travels and in furthering his mission in Alaska.

Abraham's family in Western Alaska from early 1900s

(left to right) *Abraham's grandfather Walter George holding "Uncle" Lott George; Great Grandmother Oscowelook and Abraham's father's oldest sister, Freeda George, in front; "Aunt Julia" holding Abraham's father, Jesse George; Grandmother Mary (Jesse's mother)*

In 2006, when the news of Ipli's sensational experience reached the scattered villages of his close and distant relatives, their curiosity and interest provided a ready open door of opportunity for him to travel to their villages to share his story. Their awareness of his past gave him instant credibility. This also provided him a free and friendly place to stay.

HUMILITY

I have further learned by personal observation and by what others have reported about him, that the post-2005, "new Abraham," in spite of his spectacular experiences and countless demonstrations of his powerful and efficacious prayers, has consistently maintained a *humble attitude*. He has consistently given credit and glory to God. In one of

168

our interviews Abraham boldly affirmed: ***"Everything that's happening is not from me—I don't claim it. It's the Lord!"*** Abraham's humility also caught the attention of Doc Nicholson who spoke of it saying:

> *"I have found Abraham to be a humble man—not seeking self-glory, but constantly and consistently giving glory and praise to God. 'All glory to the Lord Jesus Christ' is a phrase frequently on his lips."*
>
> ~BISHOP WILLIAM NICHOLSON

A LIVING MESSAGE OF HOPE

Due to his horrendous earlier lifestyle, Abraham became a powerful living demonstration of his message—a modern day "thief on the cross"—exemplifying clearly the amazing grace and limitless transforming power of God. He is a living, walking, talking message of hope to all broken, hopeless people he continues to touch.

CONCLUSION

Well, we've come to the end of our journey with the Celestial Traveler. We've traced Abraham's travels from the remote Alaskan backwoods on his "sno-go" to his speed-of-thought celestial travels to Heaven, Outer Darkness and Hell, and back to Earth.

We've attended Abraham on his mission trips crisscrossing Alaska—and in its villages declaring his story and vital heavenly message and demonstrating what he had been promised in heaven—*"When you speak, I'll be with you and the power of the Holy Spirit will be with you."* We have observed countless times the visible effects of this invisible divine power—the "wind" causing miracles, signs and wonders. A powerful spiritual wind transforming human lives—beginning with Abraham George and then countless others.

We have also traced my own journey in pursuit of the truth. I've shared with you my discoveries of the many proofs I found which eventually overcame my skepticism and led me to a strong and well-founded belief. The fundamental premise of the book is that Abraham's testimony is true and has been proven to be true by the many significant proofs which have been presented.

THE MEANING OF IT ALL

By now you likely have wondered if there might be some deeper underlying meaning or purpose to this whole amazing Abraham event, and if so, what? I have discovered that there definitely is and it is found within Abraham's own statements.

> *"Everything that's happening is not from me—I don't claim it. It's the Lord! Just like the blinking of an eye, He [Jesus] took me places... it was all by His command—I had no control. He showed me what He wants me to see... Jesus knew what's going to happen after He brings me back to my body. Jesus said: 'When you speak, I'll be with you and the power of the Holy Spirit will be with you. Everywhere you go, my Holy Spirit will be with you.'"*

From these statements I have deduced that Abraham's story is actually Jesus' story, of which Abraham is its main character. The plot, the celestial destinations, the message, the follow-up mission—were all predetermined by Jesus Himself.

In Jesus' story, Abraham was a doubly-dead man (*"I had no control"*)—on his way to Hell—his just reward. Then Jesus—for His own reasons—intervened and spared his life, giving him a second chance at life.

Then He gave Abraham the Holy Spirit—*"the power of the Holy Spirit will be with you"*—to empower him to accomplish his vital mission.

Abraham's celestial travels were also clearly pre-planned and guided by Jesus Himself—*"Just like the blinking of an eye, He (Jesus) took me places... it was all by His command... He showed me what He wants me to see."*

All of Abraham's mission travels, astounding acts and accomplishments were also not of his own doing. Abraham indicated that Jesus had told him: *"I'm going to bring you to places where you never even thought of going."* Abraham also said: *"Everything that's happening is not from me—I don't claim it. It's the Lord!"*

The message Abraham brought back from heaven was also given to him by Jesus. That message is essentially about Jesus Himself—His true identity, His mission and His imminent return to earth. It is a sober warning **TO BE READY**. I concur with Melvin Andrew's assessment: *"I have only to believe what I saw. I can only say, Jesus is Lord and Abraham is now an apostle[1] to us, with a specific message from the Lord Jesus Christ himself."*

My Final Appeal

If you still find yourself wavering about whether you believe Abraham's testimony is true, I want to encourage you to experience his live presentation—**the very one** that in 2008, hooked me and drew me into becoming a participant in Abraham's ongoing and developing saga. You may view that video at www.celestialtraveler.org.

Abraham's Final Appeal

I have deferred to Abraham to speak the final word since he is the one who has "been there" and can speak with experiential authority:

"There are so many things that Jesus showed me, but these are more important for me to tell. The Lord took me there so I could warn His children those places are real! Jesus told me: 'Tell my children there's heaven and hell. Tell my children I am the way, the truth, and the life and no man comes to the Father, except through me.' He told me to tell His children that He's coming soon—sooner than they think. He said this three times, each time louder and louder. Jesus told me He's at the door and looking at His Father. He's waiting for His Father's command. When the Father says **'GO!'** *He's coming to get His children. 'Tell my children the world is coming to an end. Tell my children to* **get ready**.'"*

~ABRAHAM GEORGE

---

1   *Apostle: Literally, one who is sent out; a person sent by another; a messenger. (Dictionary.reference.com)*

Epilogue

"If this is from God, it will last. If not, it will go away."

~Abraham George

2006

It is now 2015 and nine years have passed since Abraham made this bold and challenging declaration before his fellow Manokotak villagers. Abraham has remained sober and steadfast and has never returned to his old ways. His wife, Eileen, also continues in her sobriety and has become Abraham's strongest supporter, frequently traveling with him to his speaking engagements. Abraham still forges ahead in his travels, proclaiming his amazing story and heavenly message wherever he is invited—"places he never even thought of going." Abraham's cell phone continues to ring several times a day and he prays for those requesting it.

I recently asked Abraham about his future and he abruptly replied: *"Still travel until He comes, because He told me, 'You've got to go to the places where I send you.'"*

On September 19, 2014, the leadership of the newly formed Alaskan Moravian denomination—"United Alaska Moravian Ministry"—conferred their special recognition of Abraham's calling and mission, declaring: *"God has given this man special gifts for ministry; he is therefore recognized and recommended as an Evangelist."*

CERTIFICATE OF RECOGNITION
An Evangelist of United Alaska Moravian Ministry

IN THE NAME OF THE TRIUNE GOD,
FATHER, SON, AND HOLY SPIRIT

This Certifies

That _____ Mr. Abraham G. George _____

is recognized and recommended as an Evangelist. God has given this man special gifts for ministry and is the bearer of the Gospel of Jesus Christ under United Alaska Moravian Ministry Group (UAMM). Recognition is granted on the 19th day of September A.D. 2014. According to God's Word, "The Evangelist Preaches the Good News (Mark 16:15) and Makes Disciples of all nations (Matthew 28:19).

In Witness Whereof, we, as a Bishop and Chairman representing UAMM, hereunto subscribed our names affirming said Recognition by the Ministry Group.

Episcopus Fratrum, President

William H. Nicholson
U A M M

Ministerial Committee, Chairman

United Alaska Moravian Ministry Certificate of Recognition of Abraham's mission and calling.

Truly a powerful spiritual wind continues to blow across Alaska and it is destined to soon reach many other places of the world—perhaps even where you live.

The "NEW" Abraham, with Eileen and their granddaughter.

174

Abraham George, evangelist

Caption: *Abraham George speaking at the 2012 Awakening Conference, Dena'ina Center, Anchorage—with an estimated 1,000 people attending from all parts of Alaska.*

APPENDICES

SUPPLEMENTAL INFORMATION

PREFACE

BIBLICAL REFERENCES TO "CELESTIAL"
Emphases added

2 PETER 2:10 NEW INTERNATIONAL VERSION (NIV)
This is especially true of those who follow the corrupt desire of the flesh and despise authority. Bold and arrogant, they are not afraid to heap abuse on **celestial** beings; …

JUDE 1:8 NEW INTERNATIONAL VERSION (NIV)
In the very same way, on the strength of their dreams these ungodly people pollute their own bodies, reject authority and heap abuse on **celestial** beings.

ISAIAH 24:21 AMPLIFIED BIBLE (AMP)
And in that day the Lord will visit and punish the host of the high ones on high [the host of heaven in heaven, **celestial** beings] and the kings of the earth on the earth.

DANIEL 10:13 AMPLIFIED BIBLE (AMP)
But the prince of the kingdom of Persia withstood me for twenty-one days. Then Michael, one of the chief [of the **celestial**] princes, came to help me, for I remained there with the kings of Persia.

2 CORINTHIANS 5:2 Amplified Bible (AMP)

Here indeed, in this [present abode, body], we sigh and groan inwardly, because we yearn to be clothed over [we yearn to put on our **celestial** body like a garment, to be fitted out] with our heavenly dwelling, ...

THE CALL OF CELESTIAL PRAISE

PSALM 148 New International Version (NIV)

¹ Praise the Lord.

    Praise the Lord from the heavens;
    praise him in the heights above.
² Praise him, all his angels;
    praise him, all his heavenly hosts.
³ Praise him, sun and moon;
    praise him, all you shining stars.
⁴ Praise him, you highest heavens
    and you waters above the skies.

⁵ Let them praise the name of the Lord,
    for at his command they were created,
⁶ and he established them for ever and ever—
    he issued a decree that will never pass away.

⁷ Praise the Lord from the earth,
    you great sea creatures and all ocean depths,
⁸ lightning and hail, snow and clouds,
    stormy winds that do his bidding,
⁹ you mountains and all hills,
    fruit trees and all cedars,
¹⁰ wild animals and all cattle,
    small creatures and flying birds,
¹¹ kings of the earth and all nations,
    you princes and all rulers on earth,
¹² young men and women,
    old men and children.

¹³ Let them praise the name of the Lord,

for his name alone is exalted;
his splendor is above the earth and the heavens.
[14] And he has raised up for his people a horn,
the praise of all his faithful servants,
of Israel, the people close to his heart.

HISTORICAL USE OF "CELESTIAL"

"I'LL FLY AWAY"
Song by: Albert E. Brumley
©1932 Hartford Music Company. Renewed 1960 Albert E. Brumley And Sons (Admin. by ClearBox Rights, LLC)

Some glad morning when this life is o'er
I'll fly away
*To a home on God's **celestial** shore*
I'll fly away

CHAPTER 6:
RETURN TO HEAVEN, COMMISSIONING, AND ANGELIC SEND-OFF

PICTURE: *"**Angelic Send-Off**: Eileen found this artist's rendition on the internet. This is very close to what Abraham saw as he was sent back to earth from heaven."*
We have searched for the creator of this artwork with no results. If any readers can provide the artist's information, we'd like to give proper attribution.

Alaska Native Medical Center

DISCHARGE SUMMARY

GEORGE, ABRAHAM

HRCN: 07-50-42

DICT: Josh K Trussell, MD

ADMITTED: 11/30/2005
DISCHARGED: 12/27/2005   ATT:

JAN 10

DIAGNOSES TREATED:
1. Multiple right rib fractures.
2. Liver laceration.
3. Pelvic fracture.
4. L3 to L4 transverse process fracture.
5. Respiratory failure from pulmonary contusion.
6. Right brachial plexus stretch.
7. Right pleural effusion.

CONSULTATIONS:
1. Nutritional therapy.
2. Respiratory therapy.
3. Physical therapy.
4. Orthopedic surgery.

PROCEDURE:
1. Right chest thoracostomy tube placed November 30, 2005.
2. Multiple epidurals for pain control.
3. Central IV lines.

CONDITION ON DISCHARGE: Good.

CODE STATUS: Full code.

HOSPITAL COURSE: This is a 43-year-old male who was medivac'd from his village area of Manokotak on November 30, 2005 after having been involved in a snow mobiling accident during which he sustained many rib fractures and the other injuries noted above the problem list. In the Alaska Native Medical Center emergency department he was thoroughly evaluated and found to have the injuries above after which he was admitted for due management of these injuries. A chest tube was placed on the right side in the emergency department to relieve a hemothorax and several days later an epidural was placed to provide pain control to allow the patient to have adequate inspiration. Nevertheless, his severe right pulmonary contusion along with poor inspiratory effort from severe pain from the rib fractures eventually led to his respiratory failure requiring intubation and transfer to the intensive care unit.

Abraham's Medical Discharge Form from ANMC
(Alaska Native Medical Center, Anchorage Alaska)

Alaska Trial Court Cases

webmaster@courts.state.ak.us

Home | CourtView Search | Pay Online with Credit Card

CourtView Help

CAUTION: This screen shows only that a case was filed. It does not show how the case ended. Do not assume that a defendant was convicted just because a criminal case was filed.

Search Criteria
Last Name: george*; **First Name:** abraham;

Search Results

37 record(s) found.

1-37 of 37   Sort Results..   Go

Party	Affl	Party Type	D.O.B	Case Status	Case Number
George, Abraham		DFNDT	03/26/1962	Closed	3AN-94-02903CR
George, Abraham		DFNDT	03/26/1962	Closed	3DI-00-00415CR
George, Abraham		DFNDT	03/26/1962	Closed	3DI-00-00485CR
George, Abraham		DFNDT	03/26/1962	Closed	3DI-01-00415CR
George, Abraham		DFNDT		Closed	3DI-90-00037SC
George, Abraham		DFNDT	03/26/1962	Closed	3DI-96-00075CR
George, Abraham		DFNDT		Closed	3DI-96-00076SC
George, Abraham		DFNDT	03/26/1962	Closed	3DI-96-00083CR
George, Abraham		DFNDT	03/26/1962	Closed	3DI-97-00496CR
George, Abraham		DFNDT	03/26/1962	Closed	3DI-98-00313CR
George, Abraham		DFNDT		Closed	4BE-01-00019CI
George,					4BE-85-

http://www.courtrecords.alaska.gov/pa/pa.urd/PAMW6500   12/31/2010

Abraham's multiple arrest records (Page 1)

Abraham	DFNDT	Closed	00420SC
George, Abraham	DFNDT	03/26/1962 Closed	4BE-86-00441CR
George, Abraham	DFNDT	Closed	4BE-89-00118SC
George, Abraham	DFNDT	03/26/1962 Closed	4BE-93-00294CR
George, Abraham	DFNDT	03/26/1962 Closed	4BE-98-00450CR
George, Abraham	DFNDT	03/26/1962 Closed	4BE-99-00638CR
George, Abraham G	DFNDT	03/26/1962 Closed	3AN-94-T793506
George, Abraham G	DFNDT	03/26/1962 Closed	3DI-00-00296CR
George, Abraham G	DFNDT	03/26/1962 Closed	3DI-01-00088CR
George, Abraham G	DFNDT	03/26/1962 Closed	3DI-04-00401CR
George, Abraham G	DFNDT	03/26/1962 Closed	3DI-04-00584CR
George, Abraham G	DFNDT	03/26/1962 Closed	3DI-05-00126CR
George, Abraham G	DFNDT	03/26/1962 Closed	3DI-05-00506CR
George, Abraham G	DFNDT	03/26/1962 Closed	3DI-05-00589CR
George, Abraham G	DFNDT	03/26/1962 Closed	3DI-05-D002086
George, Abraham G	DFNDT	03/26/1962 Closed	3DI-06-00083CR
George, Abraham G	DFNDT	03/26/1962 Closed	3DI-10-00068CR
George, Abraham G	DFNDT	03/26/1962 Closed	3DI-10-00082MO
George, Abraham G	DFNDT	03/26/1962 Closed	3DI-10-00299CR
George,			3DI-89-
Abraham G	DFNDT	03/26/1963 Closed	00259CR
George, Abraham G	DFNDT	03/26/1962 Closed	3DI-92-00237CR
George, Abraham G	DFNDT	03/26/1962 Closed	3DI-97-00562CR
George, Abraham G	DFNDT	03/26/1962 Closed	3DI-98-00020CR
George, Abraham G	DFNDT	03/26/1962 Closed	3DI-98-00415CR
George, Abraham G	DFNDT	03/26/1962 Closed	4BE-99-00233CR

Abraham's multiple arrest records (Pages 2&3)

CHAPTER 13:
THE FIVE INHERENT PROOFS IN ABRAHAM'S TESTIMONY

PROPHECIES REGARDING SPIRITUAL REVIVAL IN ALASKA

JANUARY 6, 1991

"I see a fire in Alaska. I see a fire in that whole western area of Canada and Alaska. Alaska shall be INFLAMED with the Glory of God." [1]

~BENNY HINN

MAY 22, 1997

"I saw a map of this great nation... and I saw this hand crossing the map with some lines, and I started to watch closely... the second line started in the state of Texas and went up from Texas to Michigan, Wisconsin, Indiana, and Chicago, Illinois. But something happened and this same line started to go again from Texas, and it made a turn to Montana and then from Montana to ALASKA. And dear brothers, the fire of the Holy Spirit came, fell down on Alaska in such a way that the ice and the snow started to melt. I asked, 'What can this mean?' He said, 'I am going to melt the ice and the snow and it will turn into water because the water from the snow and ice will be a mighty outpouring of rain, but not normal rain, not regular rain; the rain of the Holy Spirit.' I am prophesying in the Name of Jesus, the rain of the Holy Ghost will descend from Alaska. Then, He said, 'The divine connection between Alaska and Puerto Montt, Chile—because Alaska is in the north extreme, while Puerto Montt is in the southern most extreme—the showers will go north from Puerto Montt, and the showers will go south from Alaska and they will meet in the middle of the continent. Revival! Revival! Revival! A mighty revival of the Holy Spirit!'" [2]

~REV. HAROLD CABALLEROS

---

1   Archives for Prophecies For Alaska, Windwalkers International site: http://windwalkersinternational.org/january-6-1991-benny-hinn
2   Given at Intercessors 500, Atlanta Georgia; Archives for Prophecies For Alaska, Windwalkers International: http://windwalkersinternational.org/may-22-1997-rev-harold-caballeros

CHAPTER 14:
STRANGE OCCURRENCES

National Transportation Safety Board	NTSB ID: ANC10LA019		Aircraft Registration Number: N207DR
FACTUAL REPORT AVIATION	Occurrence Date: 02/17/2010		Most Critical Injury: None
	Occurrence Type: Accident		Investigated By: NTSB

Location/Time						
Nearest City/Place	State	Zip Code	Local Time	Time Zone		
Kwigillingok	AK	99622	1657	AST		

Airport Proximity: Off Airport/Airstrip	Distance From Landing Facility: 1

Aircraft Information Summary		
Aircraft Manufacturer	Model/Series	Type of Aircraft
CESSNA	208B	Airplane

Revenue Sightseeing Flight: No	Air Medical Transport Flight: No

Narrative

Brief narrative statement of facts, conditions and circumstances pertinent to the accident/incident:

*** Note: NTSB investigators may not have traveled in support of this investigation and used data provided by various sources to prepare this aircraft accident report. ***

On February 17, 2010, at 1657 Alaska standard time, a Cessna 208B, N207DR, sustained substantial damage during impact with terrain following takeoff from Kwigillingok Airport (GGV), Kwigillingok, Alaska. The airline transport pilot and his seven passengers were not injured. Grant Aviation, Anchorage, Alaska, was operating the aircraft under the provisions of 14 Code of Federal Regulations Part 135. Visual meteorological conditions prevailed for the flight, which was originating at the time of the accident. The intended destination was Kipnuk, Alaska, and a company flight plan had been filed.

The pilot said that the takeoff was normal, but at 200 feet above the ground and in a turn, he observed a reduction in power. He moved the emergency fuel control lever forward, and power was restored. Before the sink rate could be reversed, the airplane impacted the surface of a frozen lake, and 5 feet of the outboard right wing was bent up. The aileron was not damaged. For safety reasons, the pilot chose to fly straight ahead for 8 miles to Kongiganak, Alaska, where the flight landed without further difficulty.

The operator's maintenance personnel inspected the engine and airframe, and determined that the right wing required a major repair to restore it to an airworthy condition. After a field repair of the right wing by the operator, the Federal Aviation Administration (FAA) granted a ferry permit for a one time flight from Kongiganak to Anchorage. The operator found no discrepancies with the engine, and it operated normally during the ferry flight.

The pilot reported to a FAA inspector that the cloud condition was 500 feet overcast with 2.5 miles visibility in light snow. There was a light wind from the north at approximately 3 to 5 knots. When the inspector asked the pilot if the airplane had ice on it when it departed Kwigillingok, he stated that there was a "trace" of ice on the wings. When interviewed by the FAA inspector, passengers made the following statements:

1. "There was freezing rain."

2. "The plane was iced up and when it took off it stalled."

3. "The weather was icing rain-.There was some ice on the wings before they took off from Kwigillingok."

There was no weather reporting facility at Kwigillingok. The closest weather reporting station was at Kipnuk, Alaska, about 26 nautical miles west of the accident site. At 1656, the reported conditions were: wind 050 degrees at 7 knots; visibility 10 statute miles; cloud condition, broken

National Transportation Safety Board:
Official Factual Aviation Report for February 17, 2010, Kwigillingok, Alaska (Page 1)

Narrative   (Continued)

at 400 feet, overcast at 3,300 feet; temperature 23 degrees Fahrenheit; dew point 23 degrees Fahrenheit; altimeter setting 29.67 inches of Mercury. The pilot told the National Transportation Safety Board's (NTSB) investigator-in-charge that the cloud condition was an indefinite ceiling at 500 to 600 feet with light snow, and the temperature was 30 degrees Fahrenheit. An NTSB meteorologist did a weather study and found that the area was subject to light snow showers, freezing fog and mist, and ground temperatures were below freezing.

The limitations section of the Cessna 208B flight manual supplement "Known Icing Equipment," states, in part: "Takeoff is prohibited with any frost, ice, snow, or slush adhering to the wings, horizontal stabilizer, vertical stabilizer, control surfaces, proper blades, or engine inlets." The limitations section also includes the following: "WARNING, EVEN SMALL AMOUNTS OF FROST, ICE, SNOW OR SLUSH ON THE WING MAY ADVERSELY CHANGE LIFT AND DRAG. FAILURE TO REMOVE THESE CONTAMINANTS WILL DEGRADE AIRPLANE PERFORMANCE AND MAY PREVENT A SAFE TAKEOFF AND CLIMBOUT."
Updated on Apr 12 2011 1:47PM

National Transportation Safety Board	NTSB ID: ANC10LA019	
FACTUAL REPORT AVIATION	Occurrence Date: 02/17/2010	
	Occurrence Type: Accident	

Weather Information

WOF ID	Observation Time	Time Zone	WOF Elevation	WOF Distance From Accident Site	Direction From Accident Site
		AST	Ft. MSL	NM	Deg. Mag.

Sky/Lowest Cloud Condition:		Ft. AGL	Condition of Light: Day		
Lowest Ceiling: Overcast		500 Ft. AGL	Visibility: 2 SM	Altimeter: 29.67 "Hg	
Temperature: -5 °C	Dew Point: -5 °C		Weather Conditions at Accident Site: Visual Conditions		
Wind Direction: 360	Wind Speed: 4		Wind Gusts:		
Visibility (RVR): Ft.	Visibility (RVV) SM				

Precip and/or Obscuration:
    Light - Showers - Snow; No Obscuration

Accident Information

Aircraft Damage: Substantial	Aircraft Fire: None	Aircraft Explosion None

- Injury Summary Matrix	Fatal	Serious	Minor	None	TOTAL	
First Pilot				1	1	
Second Pilot						
Student Pilot						
Flight Instructor						
Check Pilot						
Flight Engineer						
Cabin Attendants						
Other Crew						
Passengers				7	7	
- TOTAL ABOARD -				8	8	
Other Ground						
- GRAND TOTAL -				8	8	

National Transportation Safety Board:
Official Factual Aviation Report for February 17, 2010, Kwigillingok, Alaska
(Pages 2&3)

National Transportation Safety Board	NTSB ID: ANC10LA019	
FACTUAL REPORT AVIATION	Occurrence Date: 02/17/2010	
	Occurrence Type: Accident	

Landing Facility/Approach Information

Airport Name	Airport ID:	Airport Elevation	Runway Used	Runway Length	Runway Width
Kwigillingok Airport	GGV	18 Ft. MSL	33	2510	60

Runway Surface Type: Dirt; Ice

Runway Surface Condition: Ice; Rough; Snow

Approach/Arrival Flown: NONE

VFR Approach/Landing: None

Aircraft Information

Aircraft Manufacturer	Model/Series	Serial Number
CESSNA	208B	208B0859

National Transportation Safety Board:
Official Factual Aviation Report for February 17, 2010, Kwigillingok, Alaska (Page 4)

RESOURCES

HISTORY OF ALASKA NATIVES' LOSS OF SOCIAL & CULTURAL INTEGRITY

- ***ALASKA NATIVES COMMISSION, FINAL REPORT, Volume I***

  PART ONE: A documentation of the physical, social, and economic changes over the past two centuries that have affected the situation in which Alaska Natives find themselves today.

  PART TWO: Recommendations of the Commission in key areas… relating directly to the overarching principles of Native self-reliance, self-determination, and the integrity of Native cultures. Also included are discussions entitled "Native to Native"… presenting the issues…without unnecessary legalese or governmental jargon.

  PART THREE: Contains key statistical facts and findings of the Commission…and demographic and geographic information…

  http://alaskool.org/resources/anc/anc00.htm

Continued…

- *ALASKA NATIVES COMBATING SUBSTANCE ABUSE AND RELATED VIOLENCE THROUGH SELF-HEALING: A REPORT FOR THE PEOPLE*

Prepared for The Alaska Federation of Natives by the Center for Alcohol and Addiction Studies & The Institute for Circumpolar Health Studies, University of Alaska Anchorage, June 1999.

http://www.uaa.alaska.edu/instituteforcircumpolarhealthstudies/ caas/projects/report_afn.pdf

About the Author

Glenn Hermann was born and grew up in Minneapolis, Minnesota, graduating from Roosevelt High School in 1965. Following high school, he enlisted in the United States Army, spending his entire military career in Alaska. While serving in Alaska, he was selected to be the chauffeur for the Commanding General of U.S. Army, Alaska and married his high school sweetheart Sharolyn Johnson. He was honorably discharged in 1969.

Following his military career, Glenn earned a Bachelor's degree at Harding University in Searcy, Arkansas, graduating with honors in 1974. He then completed a Master's degree in Apologetics at Harding Graduate School of Religion in Memphis, Tennessee.

In 1980, Glenn moved his family from Minneapolis to Homer, Alaska, where he and his wife raised two sons and daughter. They recently celebrated their 47th anniversary and seventh grandchild. He currently resides in Anchorage, Alaska, where he is surrounded by all his children and grandchildren. He loves Alaska and is an avid outdoorsman and sportsman.

Glenn felt compelled to write the book when during his research he became convinced that Abraham George's out-of-body celestial experiences really happened and contained a vital message for humanity. He came to believe it was an event which had to be told to the world.

He confessed that writing *Celestial Traveler* has been the grandest, most demanding and fascinating endeavor of his 68 years, drawing upon every bit of his talent, training, and experience.

To learn more contact us at www.celestialtraveler.org.